Homework
Help from the
Library

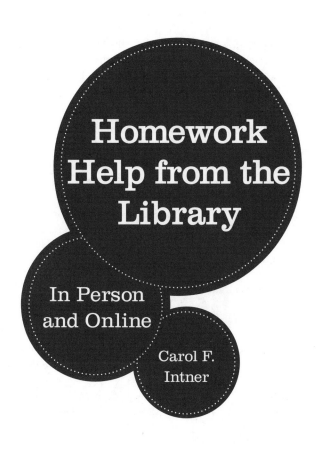

Homework Help from the Library

In Person and Online

Carol F. Intner

AMERICAN LIBRARY ASSOCIATION
CHICAGO   2011

Carol Intner is a freelance writer who has worked or volunteered in the education field for over eighteen years. She is an English teacher certified in two states, New Jersey and Maryland, where she taught ninth and tenth graders and participated in the faculty team for John F. Kennedy High School's Leadership Training Institute, a rigorous program for highly motivated students in Silver Spring, Maryland. She cofounded and coordinated an elementary school homework club for at-risk students in North Chevy Chase, Maryland, and has tutored both elementary and middle school students at their public schools in New York City, where she now resides.

Printed in the United States of America

15 14 13 12 11   5 4 3 2 1

While extensive effort has gone into ensuring the reliability of the information in this book, the publisher makes no warranty, express or implied, with respect to the material contained herein.

Note that any URLs referenced in this volume, which were valid at the time of first print publication, may have changed prior to electronic publication.

ISBN: 978-0-8389-1046-7

Library of Congress Cataloging-in-Publication Data
Intner, Carol F.
  Homework help from the library : in person and online / Carol F. Intner.
    pages cm
  Includes bibliographical references and index.
  ISBN 978-0-8389-1046-7 (alk. paper)
  1. Homework centers in libraries--United States. 2. Libraries and students--United States. 3. Homework--United States--Library resources. I. Title.
  Z718.7.I58 2011
  025.5--dc22
                                                                                              2010042096

Book design in Minion Pro and Clarendon by Casey Bayer

♾ This paper meets the requirements of ANSI/NISO Z39.48–1992 (Permanence of Paper).

ALA Editions also publishes its books in a variety of electronic formats. For more information, visit the ALA Store at www.alastore.ala.org and select eEditions.

Contents

Preface

2:40 p.m. A gaggle of high school students bursts from the building a few blocks away and spreads like an amoeba. The teenagers are energized with hormones and freedom from school rules. *No talking, sit down, line up, hands to yourself, respectful language please, take out your books, put away your cell phones.* No teachers or administrators keep watchful eyes over them once school lets out. They fight. They flirt. They egg each other on. They seem oblivious to the adults stepping aside to avoid their groups of two and three who talk and laugh too loudly.

2:55 p.m. In the elementary school yard, eighteen classes of children stand in neat double lines. Girls on one side, boys on the other. Now they are quiet because they know their classes will not be dismissed if they poke each other or tell a joke or whisper someone else's secret. But in just a few minutes, each of the K–5 classes will disperse and run to grasp the hands of waiting parents or babysitters, to climb the steps onto the school bus, or to walk the few blocks home. When all eighteen classes have been dismissed, the sound most resembles a cheering stadium full of avid football fans just as the quarterback completes the game-winning touchdown pass.

6:00 p.m. Charter school students, fifth through eighth graders, pour from the stairwell onto the street. Some walk to the train; others get rides. The official school day ends at 4 p.m., but all students are required to participate in afterschool activities four days a week. For some this means tutoring; others join the dance team or chess club. They might have emerged from the building like students elsewhere—a tumble of laughter, games, and teasing—except for one thing: they have been in the same building since 7:30 a.m. and they are exhausted.

7:30 p.m. The basketball game has ended and the visiting team won. Coach tells the players where they made their mistakes and what they need to do to improve. His screaming, loud enough to make them cringe, is interspersed with gentle encouragement. However he modulates his voice, the girls stare at the floor.

What do the hormone-laden high school student, the wide-eyed elementary school student, the exhausted middle school student, and the demoralized athlete have in common? They all have homework assignments. And they're coming to your library, either in person or via the Internet. This guide will help you prepare for them.

Introduction

IN 2001, CINDY MEDIAVILLA published the seminal *Creating the Full-Service Homework Center in Your Library.* Advocating the development of formal homework programs, Mediavilla pointed out the potential for homework programs to solve a range of problems associated with unattended children after school, from the children's vulnerability to dangerous influences to the mayhem that accompanies the large numbers of school-age patrons who converge on libraries. Her book remains the quintessential guide to the practicalities of setting up a formal homework help center to provide one-on-one homework assistance to student patrons.

Ten years later, students continue to turn to the library for help with homework, and the plethora of choices for how to provide that assistance is expanding rapidly as the types of communication and information delivery vehicles increase: web pages, databases, the Internet, Facebook, Twitter, IM-ing. Formal homework programs continue to operate successfully, but they cannot possibly satisfy all the homework-related information and educational needs of young patrons—and this is an especially critical time for librarians to meet those needs. Today we have the vast majority of an entire generation raised with access to huge amounts of information at their fingertips without ever leaving their homes. If libraries have young people within their walls or on their websites today, and the interest of those young people is primarily homework help, then staff must use this opportunity to get kids hooked on libraries so they become the adult patrons of tomorrow. Show them what libraries have to offer that home-based Internet cannot, and illustrate for them how they can benefit from their libraries wherever they may be—at the library, at home, at school, or at Starbucks.

If we accept for the moment the "conventional wisdom . . . that most children making use of [the] public library . . . are there for homework purposes" (Walter 2001, 31), we must still ask how providing homework help relates to the mission of the library outside the need to secure future patronage. To some extent the answer to this question differs depending on whether the library in question is a school media center or a public library, although in both cases providing homework supports the library's mission.

School libraries are intertwined with the educational system so that the librarian's expertise is utilized specifically to meet educational goals. School librarian and columnist Joyce Kasman Valenza appeals to teachers to take advantage of this expertise and assures them that "[school] librarians get their kicks from making you [the teacher] look good. Not only do they help learners learn, they help teachers teach" (Valenza 2007). One of the school librarian's primary roles is to support the teaching process as part of a cohesive staff with shared goals and priorities. School librarians teach students how to access information and support the implementation of school curricula. Students may be required to spend a certain amount of time each week in the library, and teachers may bring classes there to begin working on long-term homework projects or to conduct research related to specific assignments. In many school libraries, students continue this process on their own after school or during lunch. Helping students with homework in this manner is an integral aspect of the school librarian's role. However, if school administrators perceive a need for formal homework or out-of-classroom assistance, the resulting programs will probably fall under the auspices of classroom teachers, not the school librarian.

In contrast, usually the general or youth librarian in the public library operates entirely outside the context of the school structure and all that implies.[1]

The public library's constituency is the community at large, and the stated purpose of the library varies from facility to facility. Rather than adopt a professionwide mission for libraries, the Public Library Association (PLA) publishes *Planning for Results,* which includes a list of "service responses" from which library planners can pick and choose depending on needs in their communities. "Formal learning support," the response applicable to homework assistance, refers to helping students with formal education, whether those students are educated at home or enrolled at a public or private school or university. Although this may be one of many service options, both librarians and patrons believe it to be an important component of the public library's mission, a view shared by teachers, parents, and community leaders. However, the underpinning of the library's role in educating students is quite different from the foundation of classroom education. The librarian participates in education to respond to the needs and wishes of the library patron, not to improve test scores or because a school administrator insists on it to reach assessment objectives. The general or youth librarian has the opportunity to instruct patrons with every interaction—all of which are voluntary on the part of the student—but it is not the main thrust of those interactions. These librarians do not give assignments, and the intent behind their questions is to determine how the patron can best find the desired information, not to check how well the student recalls a recently taught concept.

Thus, the public librarians' role differs from that of their school counterparts in the planning, implementation, and oversight of homework assistance, but not in the mandate to provide it. Students want assistance with their homework, and helping kids with homework is part of the mission of children's and youth services in all libraries serving the needs of school-age children. The question that remains, and the focus of this book, is how to do it effectively.

Any cogent homework assistance program or set of programs should be based on current advances in information services *and* progress in the field of education. Just as research in information services has helped librarians learn to retrieve and deliver information effectively and provide a range of services in library buildings, pedagogy utilizes research to determine how children learn and how best to help them do so. Therefore, instead of forcing librarians to reinvent the wheel when they interact with students, especially when they are providing homework help, knowledge of productive pedagogical methods can inform successful homework help in libraries.

In effect, homework help should be the confluence of the education and information service fields. I address this concept in the first chapter of the book. A discussion about the history of youth services and patterns of library usage is followed by an examination of recent developments in education and a comparative analysis of education and library service methods involving children. In chapter 2, I outline the menu of services from which the librarian can choose to develop a homework assistance program and considerations for selecting from that menu. Mediavilla explored one option in her book: one-on-one tutoring centers. Librarians can, however, employ many other techniques depending on the parameters of a library's homework help program. The topic of chapter 3 is staff input and training, which are critical to the success of any program you implement in the library. Changes in technology affecting communication and information services are so numerous and occur so rapidly that I devote two chapters to them: chapter 4, to explore using in-house technology in homework help programs, and chapter 5, in which the discussion centers on patrons using technology from remote locations. Chapter 6 addresses using pedagogical techniques to answer homework reference queries effectively, and I cover troubleshooting in chapter 7. Once you have established a productive set of homework help services, if you cannot convince school children to use them, it does not matter how good they are, and if they are not meeting the needs of your patrons, you have to go back to the drawing board. Therefore, the final two chapters cover two important administrative functions: marketing and evaluation.

Note
1. Dozens of libraries across the United States are housed in school buildings to further the cooperative relationship between the school and the library, and in at least one case, the city of Nashville, the mayor wants the public library system to operate all school media centers as well (Goldberg 2009).

ONE

Background
Homework Help as the Confluence of Information Services and Education

E VERY BUILDING REQUIRES a foundation, and this chapter is the foundation for this book. Information services and education have parallel histories driven by similar—sometimes even the same—events and often the same cultural problems and priorities. Yet the research and training for each of these fields are conducted in entirely separate domains, with only a bit of overlap. Neither field seems to suffer tremendously from the division. Where homework help in libraries is concerned, however, education and information services fully entwine—sometimes creating knots in the process. Homework assignments are designed by teachers to support the learning process and meet school objectives. Teachers are trained in pedagogical techniques that help them create assignments and work with students, but still students are often overwhelmed by their homework. They, in turn, come to libraries or their websites for information and assistance, but the library staff, expert in information services, may be less familiar with pedagogical strategies that can inform and improve the services they provide to students. The purpose of this book is to review the range of services from which librarians can choose to plan their homework help programs and outline pedagogical techniques that can facilitate the process and enhance face-to-face—or computer-to-computer—encounters between librarians and their young patrons. The purpose of this chapter is to outline the background and context for the practical approaches explored in the remainder of the text.

The discussion begins with a brief review of youth services, specifically as it relates to helping students with homework. How much do kids actually use the library, though? Does their usage pattern warrant this exploration of how to help them with homework? These questions are answered in an examination of the available information on youth usage of libraries. A brief history of pedagogical trends and advances follows, with an emphasis on learning style theory because it has powerful practical implications for providing homework help. The chapter closes with a short perusal of common ground: the shared priorities and formal cooperative programs between libraries and schools, and formal homework programs in library buildings.

GENERAL HISTORY OF YOUTH SERVICES

Mention "youth services" and "libraries" to anyone uninvolved in the information services world, and the listener, searching for a personal way to connect to the topic, will respond with a tale about bringing a toddler to the local library's story hour, or how his ninth-grade daughter feels about the required, graded session in the school media center, or the value of summer reading programs, or a teenager's wonder that her local library hosts game nights. "Youth services," though it sounds like a cohesive set of programs, is characterized by a wide range of functions for a diverse clientele. As Christine Jenkins (2000, 103) writes in her survey of research on youth services librarianship, "youth service librarianship—a term that encompasses all library services to youth (children and young adults, ages zero to eighteen) in school and public library settings—has long been considered the classic success story of American libraries." Despite the dearth of research on long stretches of youth services' history that Jenkins and other experts lament, certain events of significance and trends in serving young patrons emerge in the historical record.

Gaining Entrance: The Earliest Years of Youth Services

Today it is hard to imagine a library without young patrons, but the first libraries in the United States, the Harvard College library established in 1638 and Ben Franklin's Philadelphia Library Company founded in 1732, did not welcome kids. By the nineteenth century, however, the idea that children should have access to libraries—at least to *some* libraries—took shape. In 1803, author, publisher, and bookseller Caleb Bingham donated 150 books for a children's library in his hometown of Salisbury, Connecticut, and "apprentice libraries" for working young men were established in Philadelphia and Brooklyn in 1820 and 1823, respectively. The goal of these libraries was to help the patrons further their education, and, for the most part, library usage was limited to young men (the Brooklyn library did permit girls to use the library one afternoon a week). A few years later, the towns of Peterborough, New Hampshire, and West Cambridge, Massachusetts, opened children's libraries. At the same time, various churches developed libraries for Sunday school students. To attract poor children to participate, not only were the books lent out for free, but eventually secular material was included, too.

Misgivings about allowing children into libraries continued through most of the 1800s even as services to youth were expanding. A pivotal event cited in many histories of children's services is the 1835 New York State legislation to fund libraries within each school district. But these libraries were intended for the use of adults, not the children who attended school (Sayers 1963). In the last quarter of the nineteenth century, the ambivalence to allowing children in libraries changed, and in short order children's services were among the most important provided. In 1876, when it was common for libraries to be closed to children below high school age, the U.S. Bureau of Education produced the report "Public Libraries in the United States of America," in which William Fletcher made the argument that age restrictions should be eliminated and special facilities for children provided in libraries throughout the country. At the very first ALA conference, Samuel S. Green gave a presentation that included a discussion of assisting young patrons, and three years later the conference theme was children's literature. Public discourse began on the nature and quality of literature available to children. However, as Sayers (1963, 8) points out, "not until twenty years later did the persistent knocking of children upon the doors of libraries succeed." In the last decade of the nineteenth century, circulating library rooms for children began to open throughout the country. Services to children expanded to include story hours, games, and reading clubs, and at the turn of the century, training programs for children's librarianship opened at Pratt Institute in Brooklyn and the Carnegie Pittsburgh Training School.

The Modern Library Movement: The First Half of the Twentieth Century

From the very inception of the "modern library movement" with the creation of ALA, the necessity for a cooperative relationship between libraries and schools was recognized. ALA appointed a committee to work with teachers'

National Education Association to improve public education, and school libraries, as they are currently configured, developed out of early public library service to schools of the late 1890s and early 1900s (Jenkins 2000, 107). In 1901, Josephine Rathbone provided a history to date of the relationship between schools and libraries, including the 1879 ALA conference that brought teachers and librarians together to discuss mutual needs for the first time, and several cooperative programs were implemented in the late 1870s (Rathbone 1901). At that 1879 conference, R. C. Metcalf, headmaster of the Wells School in Boston, openly expressed at least one obstacle to that process: antipathy among some educators for the library: "It remains to suggest how, in my opinion, the public library can be made a great public benefit, rather than what it frequently is, a public nuisance. So long as our pupils are allowed free access to a public library without direction as to choice, either by parent, teacher, or librarian, we can look for no good results" (quoted in Rathbone 1901).

In the early years of youth services, the majority of the information on how schools and libraries could work together focused on training students to use the library and its collection selection, and helping teachers with materials to support pedagogy rather than helping students with individual assignments. The idea of the library as a source of homework help as we know it today had not yet been hatched.

In the early twentieth century, youth services flourished. In the 1920s and '30s, the number of separate reading rooms and services for students expanded. In 1930, Effie Power wrote the first textbook for youth services librarians, *Library Service for Children,* in which she covers everything ranging from the history of youth services to which kind of furniture to use in the children's area and how to arrange it. She describes youth services as a junior varsity library experience: librarians should teach students how to use the library so they will be prepared to use adult libraries when they are older. She also highlights high standards of collection selection (no dime store novels here), cooperative relationships with schools, and helping students become knowledgeable. She touches on homework help when she includes helping students find books to read for assignments in her discussion of the youth services librarian's activities (Power 1930).

The 1930s saw a commitment to provide services for young people endorsed by library after library across the country, accompanied by an increasing awareness of the separate needs of young adults. In 1941 the ALA Division of Library Service to Children and Young People was formed, including sections for both school and public libraries. Ten years later, the Division split into several groups, one representing services for young adults (Young Adult Services Division, now called the Young Adult Library Services

Association, YALSA), and one representing librarians providing services for children (Association of Library Services to Children, ALSC). Despite these increasing attempts at cooperation between libraries and schools, public and school librarians were often at odds with each other, competing for programming and funding, and this led to the creation of a third division, the American Association of School Librarians (AASL).

The Baby Boomers and Social Change

During the 1960s, the changing political scene in the United States was reflected within the information services community. Just as the civil rights movement was gaining momentum in the country at large, in 1960, a group of African American students refused to leave a segregated library in Danville, Virginia. Sensitivity to the needs of minorities and the economically disadvantaged led to the development of community outreach programs in libraries and the expansion of collections to be more responsive to diverse users. Some libraries received funding through President Lyndon Johnson's War on Poverty, and the Elementary and Secondary Education Act of 1965 provided funding to purchase library materials and textbooks. Though some of the programs that proliferated were abolished when federal funding dried up, some best practices developed during this era remain intact, such as outreach programs and cooperation with the local community.

Throughout the 1950s and '60s, libraries were overwhelmed by huge numbers of young people in their buildings. Baby boomers began utilizing library services in greater numbers, for two reasons: there were simply more of them, and they went to libraries more often because they had more assignments. In response to the belief that education in the United States should be beefed up to make the country globally competitive, curricula—and the resulting homework—were intensified. Accommodating the large number of young people strained librarian's budgets, time, space, and patience, and some felt it detracted from adult services (Willet 1995). Some libraries resorted to refusing to answer teenagers' reference questions, eliminating or restricting borrowing and reading room privileges for young people, and requiring permission from either parents or teachers before allowing use of the library. School children got the message; in *A Fair Garden and the Swarm of Beasts,* young adult librarian Margaret A. Edwards noted that "one of the greatest barriers to full public library service was the poor attitude of public librarians towards students" (Mediavilla 2001, viii).

Exacerbating the situation, animosity between school and public librarians resurfaced when general librarians blamed school librarians for the young crowds; if the school librarians were doing their job, so the logic went, the students would not have to use public library facilities. To this day, "many public librarians feel that curriculum-based library services are best left to the schools" (Mediavilla 2001, viii). Also, the effort required to handle large crowds of students remains a concern. In fact, as recently as 2007 one library, the Maplewood (New Jersey) Memorial Library, temporarily closed its doors altogether after school hours rather than let large numbers of middle school students cross the threshold (Kelley 2007).

Technology Takeover: The 1980s through the Present

Advances in technology affecting information services dramatically impacted all information services, including youth services, in the final quarter of the twentieth century. In the 1960s catalogs began going electronic in a few pioneering libraries with mainframes, and as early as 1971 ALA's Young Adult Services Division presented a preconference event to discuss the impact of audiovisual materials on young adults. More and more catalogs began switching over to electronic format during the 1980s, when personal computers became available, and libraries began offering computer access. Through the 1980s and '90s, reference services began to include access by telephone, then e-mail, and finally IM chatting formats manned either by librarians or by private contractors. By the early twenty-first century, most public libraries offered data subscription services to all users and had web pages on the Internet, many with links for remote access to library services. Most of these libraries had a web link to a page reserved for youth services, and sometimes they offered separate pages for children and for teens. In 1997 the federal government passed the Library Services and Technology Act (LSTA) to fund technology development and access to electronic communication for under-served populations.

Youth Services and Homework Help

As Willet (1995, 97) notes, "over the course of the last hundred years, the goals and techniques of youth services have maintained a remarkable consistency. Youth librarians have concentrated on supplementing formal education and promoting self development through leisure reading and activities." Some form of homework assistance has always been part of this youth services legacy, and today homework assistance of one kind or another is a standard service to young people. In the early years, collection development was driven by local school curricula, and as youth services began to develop and expand, many shared the viewpoint expressed by the Massachusetts Board of Library Commissioners and Bureau of Library Extension in a 1968 policy statement: "Neither the school nor the public library alone can provide the quality and the quantity of materials necessary to serve all the demands of the curriculum and the community" (Woolls 2003, 528). By the mid-1980s, some libraries in California had established formal homework assistance programs, and increasingly libraries across the country have implemented such programs. In the very beginnings of youth services, libraries supplemented formal education. Now libraries have become an integral part of the education process.

Patterns of Youth Usage of the Library

To what extent should libraries accommodate the preferences of young users? Theoretically and practically, it is important to meet the needs of school-age users now so that future patronage will be secure. This is especially critical in the age of the Internet. However, even beyond this nugget of common sense, the small amount of available statistics about library usage warrants taking note of and responding to young patrons. They are *who* is using the library; therefore we must determine *how* they use the library and help them do so.

In virtually all research on youth library usage, studies show that the vast majority of children and young adults use libraries and constitute the largest proportion of the library user population. In the 1981, a survey in Canada found that 90 percent of young adults surveyed used the library at least occasionally. A slightly later study in Calgary found that 82 percent of children in fourth through sixth grade used the library within the previous year, whereas only 50 percent of adults could make that claim. A 1989 survey in Rock County, Wisconsin, confirmed this pattern, if not the precise numbers: almost 68 percent of all youths had used the library in the previous year, including 86.5 percent of all twelve- to fourteen-year-olds. Of the latter group who used the library, a little over half reported using it more than ten times each year (statistics from Willet 1995).

The most recent statistics available are compelling. The U.S. Department of Education found that children and young adults constitute 60 percent of library users on any given day; 37 percent are children, and almost one library user in four is a young adult. Furthermore, the ethnic and racial makeup of children in libraries had changed; 40 percent of librarians reported that diversity increased over the five years preceding the survey (Collins and Chandler 1997). Examining library usage by polling children and young adults, an ALA-funded Harris poll revealed that 88 percent of students ages eight through eighteen visited either their school or public library in person or via the Internet at some point in the previous year; nine in ten did so at least a few times a year, and about one in seven utilized library services "a couple of times a week" (Harris Interactive 2007). Young people of many backgrounds use both their school and public libraries frequently, and youth are the overwhelming majority of patrons in public libraries. But what do they do while they are there? Why do they go to libraries?

The top draw of the library, whether online or in buildings, is help with school assignments and access to technology. Although patrons do report that they come to the library to find books to read for pleasure or to pursue further information in areas of personal interest, numerous studies involving student patrons in various age groups show that students come to the library to work. They go to the library for materials to complete school assignments. They want access to computers, and they want training to use those computers effectively for schoolwork. Most youth services librarians know that students head right for the computers when they enter the building, but Harris Interactive found that only a quarter of them say they use library computers for entertainment; most of them use the technology for their schoolwork rather than for activities unrelated to school or studying. Often student contact with the library consists of going to the library website for help with research and information for school assignments. As library websites become increasingly elaborate portals for finding homework information, 50 percent of all teens report going online via a library website. The implication is that there is huge potential for the impact of libraries on remote research for homework assignments. Ninety-four percent of students ages 12 to 17 use the Internet for school research, and 78 percent believe the Internet helps them complete assignments effectively (Bilal 2007).

Another way of examining how students are using libraries is to listen to what they say they would like to see improved or expanded. Some requests made in various surveys are unrelated to the nature of library usage. For example, Noelle Egan, electronics research librarian at Drexel University, analyzed the literature on young adult responses and found that kids always requested food. Students also wanted more dedicated space in libraries, fewer restrictions, and friendlier librarians (Egan 2003). In the Harris poll, young patrons nine years old and up valued qualities that reflected a desire to feel more welcomed at the library. They wanted public libraries closer to their homes, longer hours, more activities, a "warm welcoming atmosphere," and a space of their own (Harris Interactive 2007). When asked to consider the substance of the services offered, students' answers supported the conclusion that they want homework help and access to technology in the library setting. For example, Elaine Meyers's study of teen focus group responses revealed that students would like more computers in libraries so wait time for access would decrease, and that students are frustrated by the lack of help they get from staff (Meyers 1999). Specifically, teens report they need more training to use technology effectively. They want assistance on long-term projects, and they want higher-quality materials to be available. Young patrons may visit libraries in person or via the Internet for leisure purposes, but research so far indicates that their main priority vis-à-vis the library is to receive help with assignments and access to computers, virtual resources, and software that can help them with school projects.

TWENTIETH-CENTURY DEVELOPMENTS IN EDUCATION

As in the world of haute couture, pedagogical hemlines rise and fall. When the hemlines are down, more traditional, teacher-centered approaches, emphasis on academic rigor, and strict "standards" prevail. Rising hemlines, or the more progressive approaches, tend to highlight the value of student-centered and student-initiated learning, flexibility in what constitutes a classroom, and flexibility in classroom instruction. The debate about which approach more effectively educates children, which began in the first half of the twentieth century, continues today. The effect of this debate on homework help in libraries is twofold: the current fashion can affect the amount and type of homework students receive and come to complete in the library; and when a new approach is "in," techniques are developed that can be used to inform the process of providing homework help in libraries.

One of the most obvious differences between the classrooms of 1900 and those of today is the physical arrangement of the room, which, in effect, reflects the underlying differences in pedagogical philosophy:

> In 1900, a teacher typically expected her students to enter and exit her classroom in unison and to spend most of their time sitting at desks bolted to the floor. Except for periods devoted to student recitation, teachers did most of the talking. . . . By the 1990s, desks were rarely attached in fixed positions and students did not march to classes. Relationships between students and teachers were decidedly more informal. (Sealander 2003, 216)

Each time the hemlines go up and down from progressive to traditional and back again, it seems that tidbits from the "old" ways stick and are folded into the new fashions.

The First Glimmers of the Student-Centered Classroom

The concept of student-centered learning first achieved popularity in the 1920s. It was a complete about-face from standard teaching methods to that point. Prior to this, the teacher talked most of the time, students worked primarily as a whole group, and desks pointed the same direction—toward the board or teacher. In the student-centered classroom of the early twentieth century, like the student-centered classroom of today, the teacher relinquished the classroom stage to students to a large degree, guiding and directing from the wings. Students determined what they learned and how they learned it. Learning took place in small groups, and classrooms were arranged to facilitate this. Materials were varied, permitting students to choose from those approaches to which they felt they best responded, and students spoke at least as much as the teacher. Progressive reformers of the early twentieth century criticized and tried to abolish drills and rote memorization, warning that these methods were detrimental to students' health.

The Pendulum Swings Back and Forth

In the mid-1950s, the emphasis on standards and achievement had a brief resurgence after the nation reacted to two events: Rudolph Flesch published the now-famous *Why Johnny Can't Read,* in which he blames teaching methods for an epidemic of illiteracy in the United States, and the Russians launched Sputnik. The impact of Sputnik on the American ego in general and education in particular cannot be underestimated. As Powell (2007) points out, "though Sputnik was a relatively simple satellite compared with the more complex machines to follow, its beeping signal from space galvanized the United States to enact reforms in science and engineering education so that the nation could regain technological ground it appeared to have lost to its Soviet rival."

By the 1960s, however, the less structured approach of the early twentieth century had returned. Ramping up educational instruction was antithetical to the low-key, rebellion-filled 1960s. Instead, educational reformers began exploring alternative schools, open classrooms, and various student-friendly classroom strategies such as active learning, learning in a variety of media, and self-directed learning activities.

When educational researchers learned that SAT scores had declined along with attendance, enrollment in academic courses, and the number of homework assignments in the mid-1970s, the educational hemlines demurred to the more traditional approach yet again. Walls went back up between the classrooms, and over several decades the emphasis on standards, testing, and accountability gradually escalated, culminating with the enactment and domination of the No Child Left Behind Act in 2001. This legislation required every state to test every student, with few exceptions, to measure how effectively standards were met.[1] Now educators are incorporating and modifying child-centered methods developed in the progressive eras into rigorous academic standards, measured quantitatively as required by No Child Left Behind and other education policies under consideration for the future. Some of the buzzwords and concepts may differ slightly, but today's "cooperative learning" methods, emphasis on "critical thinking skills," and treatment of learning as a process rather than an end are approaches quite similar to those that were popular in earlier decades of the twentieth century.

Many educators now recommend a combination of student-centered approaches, which focus on how the student learns, and the traditional concerns of enhancing academic achievement as measured by tests, which focus on what knowledge the student acquires.

Learning Style Theory

One of the major advances of the progressive eras that have been incorporated into most teacher training programs is learning style theory: recognition that students learn in different ways and that teachers must respond to individual learning styles if they are to engage their pupils effectively. Research points to lack of educational success, especially among the most at-risk populations, because teachers do not recognize or respond to students' learning styles, not because the students are incapable of academic accomplishment. In contrast, students excel when the process of instruction, through varied activities, covers all learning styles, enabling them to respond to the methods that most effectively activate learning for each one of them.

One of the pioneers in examining the styles through which people learn was Carl Jung, who in the 1920s defined four ways of perceiving the world: sensing (following orderly procedures), feeling (emotional responses and spontaneity), intuition (perceiving ideas and information from abstractions), and thinking (rational thought). Most people tend to learn in combinations of these processes, Jung explained. For example, "intuitive-thinking" people are "theoretical, intellectual, and knowledge oriented," whereas sensing-feelers are "sociable, friendly, and interpersonally oriented" (Silver et al. 2000, 25–26). Some teachers still utilize Jung's framework when they plan lessons for their classes.

In the 1980s, Howard Gardner developed a different approach to learning style, one cited more frequently in education texts. He defined eight "intelligences" and suggested that each person excels at one or more of them. People learn better, therefore, when information is presented in a manner that appeals to that intelligence. The intelligences are as follows:

Verbal/linguistic—responds to language and words

Logical/mathematical—responds to rational patterns and tends to excel in math and science

Spatial—responds to visual presentations of material

Musical—responds to music and components of music (e.g., rhythm)

Body/kinesthetic—responds to touch and movement

Interpersonal—responds to social interaction

Intrapersonal—responds to inner feelings and ideas

Naturalist—responds to flora, fauna, and other aspects of nature

Those who train and supervise teachers or write methodology texts encourage educators to include assignments that respond to multiple intelligences. For example, a teacher who wants students to analyze a character in a literary text might appeal to those with refined musical intelligence by offering an assignment to create a rap song to express the feelings of a character in a literary text, a spatial choice might be to draw the character in detail, and a kinesthetic assignment might be to act out a scene that illustrates the character's qualities.

A more succinct learning style theory that has been widely applied was devised by special educator Grace Fernald in the 1940s: VAKT (visual, auditory, kinesthetic, and tactile learning styles). The method, which is still used with special-education students, is applied in almost every content area with learners of all grades and ability levels, including adults. The process began when Fernald used all three of the VAKT senses to teach spelling. She wrote the words down so students could see them (visual learning), had the students recite the words aloud so they could hear them (auditory learning), and then had student write the words by tracing over the letters (kinesthetic and tactile learning). Prescriptions for how best to engage different kinds of learners and types of appropriate activities for each of the VAKT senses have been extrapolated from Fernald's work, and textbooks and web pages abound with related suggestions for enhancing classroom instruction. Here are some examples of materials that best appeal to different VAKT learning styles:

For visual learners: demonstrating processes so students can watch; using photographs and pictures, charts and graphs, and study cards.

For auditory learners: describing processes aloud so students can listen; asking students to speak their answers to questions aloud; incorporating arts that involve listening, such as poetry and music.

For tactile/kinesthetic learners: asking students to write answers, either on the board or in their notebooks; incorporating student sessions at the computer to either write or retrieve information.

Almost all descriptions of best practices include utilizing some form of learning style theory or appeal to multiple intelligences, and application of this knowledge has powerful implications for anyone working with children—including librarians.

Process over Facts: Metacognitive Learning

Another set of student-centered approaches are derived from the underlying theory that students must be taught processes, or metacognitive skills, rather than knowledge. For example, in constructivist learning design, students are taught "a naturally occurring and real-world way of thinking about learning and teaching. The teacher acts as a choreographer. . . . students actively construct their own knowledge" (Gagnon and Collay 2006, xiii). Various reflective methods help students evaluate what they read. Roe et al. (2007) have outlined several of them in their text on teaching literacy across content areas. The list includes but is not limited to

Know–Want to know–Learned (KWL). Students articulate what they already know when they start a text and what they want to learn from it; then, finally, they reflect on what knowledge they have acquired.

Directed Reading/Thinking Activity (DRTA). Students think about what they already know about the subject they will examine, predict what the next portion of the text will be about, read the text, and evaluate the text by confirming, rejecting, revising, or extending their predictions.

SQ3R. Students *survey* or scan the text; develop a list of *questions* the text will likely answer; and then use 3 Rs: *read* the text, *recite* the answers to the questions developed, and *review* the material by rereading and verifying answers.

ROWAC. Students *read* headings, *organize* by creating an outline from the headings, *write* down predictions about what they are learning, *actively* read, and *correct* predictions.

At least one method, SQRQCQ (*survey, question, read, question, compute, question*), focuses on math instruction. Many of these processes qualify as "scaffolding," a current buzzword in pedagogy that refers to creating structures that help students understand how to approach material with which they struggle.

Interpersonal Relations in Education Theory

A body of research on the most effective ways to interact with students proves useful to the reference interview and other homework help processes. Those most applicable to helping students with homework in the library are addressed in detail in chapter 6. Topics range from questioning—both asking and answering questions—to constructive uses of praise and culturally responsive education. The latter is especially important because librarians have seen an increase in diversity among young patrons and must respond to their needs. Glasgow et al. (2006) identify strategies that are based on research and have proved effective in diverse classrooms, including the importance of developing personal relationships with students. Students of all backgrounds flourish when teachers establish a good rapport with them, but research shows that personal connections are especially important for enhancing classroom interactions with students from diverse communities.

Too Much, Too Little, or Just Right: The Amount of Homework and Where Libraries Fit In

Most of the theories and methods described here apply to classroom pedagogy, though they have applications to out-of-school learning. Quite a bit of the discourse on homework is about its place in the educational process, whether children have too much or too little of it, and what kinds of assignments teachers should distribute to their charges. Should students have more homework? Is homework destroying the family? Who wants homework anyway? How much is too much?

The debate about appropriate levels of homework has raged about as long as schools have been in session, but there are constants. For one, the popularity or unpopularity of homework has consistently reflected trends in education. When progressive methods that foster flexibility and open education have been in vogue, homework has been blamed for everything from poor student health (even mortality) to the devastation of the family unit. Conversely, when the tides shift and the educational guiding principle is academic excellence, the dearth and quality of homework come under fire. In fact, Gill and Schlossman (2004) found that homework levels really have not varied much from one decade to the next; what has changed is "the proportion of high school students doing 2 hours or more daily." Additionally, parents have consistently wanted their children to have homework even when no evidence exists to support the position that it helps learning; parents believe "that children who did homework learned more" (11).

From the librarian's perspective, the issue is not whether students get too much or too little homework but rather how to provide the assistance students need completing it—and they *do* need help. Not only do students frequently struggle with their homework, many need help with their assignments because often adults are not home to assist them. The library is one of the places they go when help is not available at home. If large numbers of students converge on libraries for assistance with assignments, librarians need to be ready to manage their numbers and their questions. The potential impact librarians can have on patrons is enormous, especially among those least likely to receive homework support at home. As Kralovec and Buell (2001) point out, homework is "the great discriminator" because it remains an integral aspect of educational achievement, but the factors contributing to students' ability to complete their homework well vary widely, including the amount of support their families can provide, their home environments, whether they work or play sports after school, and what supplemental resources are available to them. If librarians establish a successful menu of homework help services for students, they have the opportunity to level the playing field.

COMMON GROUND: WHERE LIBRARIES AND SCHOOLS MEET

This discussion is primarily theoretical, but these are theories that have applications to youth services as well as pedagogy, and specific suggestions for applying them to homework help in the library are presented in later chapters in the book. Some current pedagogical best practices, such as cooperative learning groups of students, are impractical in the library setting, but many of the techniques employed in the classroom can be applied to homework help in the library. Not only can schools and libraries share methods of helping their charges, but they have other similar concerns and priorities.

Literacy

Information services and education share certain priorities and experience that impact youth services. First and foremost, schools, which are in the business of teaching children to read, and libraries, the guardians of information and books, have always been concerned with literacy. In recent years, promoting literacy has become a hot topic in the professions associated with both of these fields.

Libraries were at the forefront of literacy training as early as the turn of the century, when they became involved in assisting new immigrants to read English. They also play "a major role in helping children to read. Previous evaluations of libraries, however, have often bypassed the part libraries play in improving children's literacy skills" (Celano and Neuman 2001, 4). Now libraries have gone even further in responding to current educational trends. Not only do they fulfill their traditional role of supporting literacy, they have developed programs to foster "emergent literacy," which begins before kids go off to school. Preschool programs in libraries have proliferated, as have summer reading programs that support these ends. Jones (2007, 9) advocates a similar emphasis for young adult services: "What all teen readers have in common is that they are developing a relationship with reading. The essential role of the young adult librarian is to nurture that relationship." One of the service responses YALSA suggests for its members is to support basic literacy so students can be prepared to function in their daily lives. Jones and Shoemaker (2001, 110) suggest that libraries respond to this need with "materials, tutors, and instructional software, . . . after-school, weekend, and outreach programs promoting literacy."

The field of education has also seen a broadened interest in bolstering literacy. No Child Left Behind encourages literacy instruction for all grades and provides a significant level of funding for literacy initiatives for early elementary school students. Literacy instruction is now included in most teacher education programs for all grade levels and subject areas. Now every teacher teaches reading, not just the language arts or English teacher.

In the twenty-first century, not only is literacy in general a priority for libraries and schools, but the two institutions share an interest in particular in information literacy. Information literacy is at the very heart of library service, and the proliferation of technological advances and all that implies for accessing information have resulted in increased concern about students' facility with technology in both library services and education. Teachers, librarians, general information websites, and even the government advise parents to help their children access information from different sources and to evaluate the information they access. Arguments are even being made for the inclusion of information literacy courses in teacher preparation programs at all levels of education, including college, and formal programs for teaching information literacy to students of all ages are proliferating. Similarly, as early as 1993 the AASL began recommending that information literacy be included in school curricula.

Parental Involvement

Education and information services have additional current interests of professional concern in common, such as the role of parents in providing their services. For example, parents are becoming increasingly involved in their children's education and are encouraged to do so because of the positive impact it has on academic performance. Similarly, parents are becoming more involved in their children's library experience as they bring them to participate in preschool programs, story hours, and, of course, increased homework help. In response, some librarians accommodating multiple needs within families have set up programs in which children get help with schoolwork while parents get assistance with their needs, such as learning English. Even a decade ago, Felt (1999) wrote that parents "cannot just drop off their kids in the children's area to browse. . . . Oh no, we must encourage parents to share the excitement of indexes, controlled vocabulary, and LC vs. Dewey." There was a time when students walked to the local library on their own, parents' involvement in schoolwork was limited, and assignments were created with this understanding in mind. The intentional involvement of parents and families in the worlds of youth services and education is a relatively new development.

Numbers and Accountability

In recent decades, both libraries and schools have faced the power of statistics and felt the pressure to implement an empirically based measurement process and prove their worth according to that process. In both the information services and education fields, standards, service evaluations, and some degree of accountability have been important since early on in their modern histories. Most of the criteria then, as now, are driven by professionals and researchers striving for high standards. However, an accountability movement pertaining to a multitude of public services has also had powerful affects on schools and libraries. The occasional standardized testing of pupils in the 1950s and '60s gave way to frequent, and sometimes legally mandated, testing in the 1970s through the present day. States have scrambled to meet the testing requirements of No Child Left Behind, which only recently came under criticism by researchers who question its effectiveness in closing the achievement gaps it aims to eliminate (Glasgow et al. 2006). Meanwhile, a similar trend has affected the library services world. Only a few states have not implemented standards for library service, and increasingly states are requiring libraries to meet certain criteria in order to obtain state aid. Both schools and libraries now have to justify to their constituencies that they meet their communities' needs.

*   *   *

Homework help is the place where all of the concerns mentioned in this chapter converge. It is where the history and development of youth services intersect with the history and development of K–12 education. When K–12 students descend upon libraries for assistance with school assignments, they increase library usage and beg the question of what kinds of programs should be provided to respond to their needs. Homework help is where we see the fallout of increased pressure on educators to achieve higher test scores. Educators are assigning more and more kinds of homework assignments. Then, as library patrons, students log onto library websites, seek out reference services, and struggle to navigate the stacks and the Internet to complete their schoolwork. It is where some of both the internally and externally driven priorities for each field manifest themselves in practical terms.

Many libraries have responded to this situation by implementing formal homework help programs, a form of library-subsidized tutoring. These programs involve students coming to the library after school to receive one-on-one or small-group assistance with homework assignments on specific days, sometimes as many as four days a week. In fact, some libraries have coordinated with educators to match students with a county- or district-certified teacher to answer homework questions. One example is the Chicago Public Library's privately funded "Teacher in the Library" program that operates in many branches. In her book on formal homework programs, Mediavilla (2001) advocates increasing the availability of formal in-library homework programs and provides a detailed description of how to do so.

The need for assistance with school assignments, however, is unlikely to be fully met at the library during specified school hours, especially since students' access to information is no longer dependent on a trip to the library. Now most libraries offer other options to struggling students, and those options are the focus of this book. Students still utilize regular in-library materials and reference services, and they access both reference and homework services through newer technologies such as telephone, e-mail, and chat reference services; library websites that include study advice or links to useful Internet sites; and homework hotlines. Every youth services librarian or general librarian providing services to children faces the decision of how best to provide homework help to young patrons. Aside from homework centers, many choices are available. Effective youth services in your library require a well-thought-out plan of action. Chapter 2 will assist you in that process by discussing the available options and how to evaluate them in the context of your library's needs.

Note
1. At this writing, nine years later, No Child Left Behind is under scrutiny and President Obama has announced his intention to work with Congress to revamp federal education policies.

TWO

First Steps
Planning Your Homework
Help Menu of Services

EVERY DAY, PEOPLE of all kinds stream through the doors of the diner on the corner of 100th Street and Broadway in Manhattan. Waiters know exactly what the "regulars" want without asking, arriving at tables with tea or coffee in hand; the act of offering the menu is a formality. The rest of the clientele include ambitious professionals, workers from nearby construction sites, taxi cab drivers, high school and college students, parents with small children, tourists from a nearby hotel and a hostel, and a smattering of men and women stooped with age. But each seems satisfied, and this diner has a great reputation. The menu is extensive enough that the toddler who refuses to eat anything but scrambled eggs is as happy with his meal as his mother who orders baked salmon. Compared with many local diners, the menu is more limited, yet the booths are almost always jammed. The owners have figured out who they serve and what they want. Like the diner's owner, library administrators and youth librarians intent on creating effective homework programs need to figure out who they serve and what they want. The diner has created a successful menu to respond to its customers' needs. It is incumbent on the designers of a successful library homework help program to do the same. And both menus should be designed with customer service in mind.

Planning library programming according to a customer service model has become increasingly popular over the past couple of decades. Jones and Shoemaker (2001) devote a good deal of their book on library service to teenagers to convincing their readership to look at young patrons as customers. They begin with a definition of customer service—and a word of caution:

> "Customer service" is a combination of all the ways organizations give their users what they want and keep them happy. It is user-centered, not organization-centered behavior, communication and attitudes. . . . Giving good customer service does not mean doing *anything* customers want, [but] it also does not mean blaming customers for the organization's inadequacies—sort of like, "If we don't have it, you don't want it." (5)

The needs of young patrons who come to the library for homework help vary so widely that meeting them by responding with customer service principles is a challenge for even the most diligent of youth librarians. Students in the library or on its website come from diverse backgrounds and have disparate abilities to articulate their needs. Some may struggle with English at the same time as they struggle with their homework. Some who request assistance will be more facile with computers than most teachers and librarians, while others have sat down in front of a computer only a handful of times. Some are looking for one or two pieces of information, while others need help with the researching process. Most exude urgency as they try to meet approaching homework assignment deadlines and keep up with ever-accelerating school instruction. They need the information *now*. The types of assignments these diverse students receive each day vary as well. Some wave before you a detailed rubric for a history research project; others need to practice basic algebra functions. All the while your patrons arrive from varying circumstances with a range of assignments, the technologies used to access and retrieve the information necessary to help them is changing so rapidly that keeping up with the latest developments can seem daunting. How do you begin?

NEEDS ASSESSMENT

The first step in the planning process for any library program is to conduct an accurate needs assessment. Only after you have determined exactly what your clients need can you define your program's objectives in the context of your larger institutional goals and choose a basic philosophy or approach that will help you attain your objectives. The choices you make depend on several factors, including the architecture of your building, budgetary limitations, and available staffing.

"Knowledge of client group" is the first and second competency category listed by ALSC (2009) and YALSA (2010), respectively, in their most recent descriptions of expertise required for their fields. The first step in getting to know your community of young patrons is to take notice of them and observe them. A more methodical approach is required, however, to develop an effective program to meet their needs in any sphere. A proper needs assessment should be conducted. This involves a systematic evaluation of both your patrons and your library to determine what services your clients need and how you can best meet those needs. It might involve observations, surveys, and statistical analyses.

A good deal of the literature about library needs assessment applies to the big picture, that is, an entire library or library system. However, just as marketing segmentation, or targeting subsets of the customer population, proves effective in marketing plans, library needs assessment can be conducted for portions of the user population. Dimick (1995) points out youth are already a subset of library users, and various age groupings obviously constitute additional subsets. Users of particular programs can also constitute a subset, such as patrons who use or could potential use homework assistance in the library. Assessing their needs can be achieved by applying the same approaches used for larger-scale library planning.

Needs assessments can be indirect, that is, they use existing data; or they can be direct, which requires asking patrons their views or opinions. Indirect and direct needs assessments relevant to creating a menu of homework help services can be conducted in three places: the library itself, schools, and the community at large.

Needs Assessment in the Library

In the library, the sources of information on users' needs are data, staff observations, and the users themselves. Both indirect and direct sources of information are available in the library itself, and both responses to existing services and interest in additional services should be examined.

For indirect needs assessment, a good start is to take stock of what exists and consider what current users might want to see. Try to look at your services from your users' perspectives: what does a young person see when she walks through your doors? Factors to examine include the following:

Facilities. Does your library provide dedicated facilities for young patrons, such as child-friendly furniture, study areas, and a children's section? Do teens have their own area? The vast majority of libraries offer study space for students; how heavy is usage of study spaces in your library after school and on weekends? Where do students plop their backpacks on the floor and open their notebooks? Where do they congregate?

Computer availability. Does your library have computers dedicated for young patrons' use? Does your library reserve certain computers for young patrons' use either all the time or during certain hours? If so, is usage of the facilities heavy or light? According to ALA (2009b), library staffs consistently report that afterschool hours are the busiest time for library services, and especially for computer and Internet use. Is this true for your library, too?

Circulation data. Are your circulation data gathered by subject area so that you can determine whether usage of collections that reflect local curriculum is heavy? If that usage is not heavy, does the lack of interest reflect the quality or age of the collection or outside factors, such as a change in the curricula?

Reference interview analysis. Are data available in your building on the nature of reference interviews with children and young adults? If so, this information can shed light on the specific types of assignments for which patrons seek assistance through face-to-face encounters with reference staff, and planners can extrapolate the kinds of homework assistance students need most. If data are not available, the information can be created by asking staff to log whether or not student queries relate to schoolwork, and if they do, to categorize them. A simple checkoff sheet can be used to document the quantity and nature of face-to-face, telephone, and e-mail reference encounters. Which is most popular? To which subject do most questions relate?

Website use. Eighty-three percent of all libraries provide some type of online homework assistance (ALA 2009b). If your library falls into that category, are data available to help you track "hits" on homework-related web pages or links visited so you can extrapolate usage patterns of the online assistance you offer?

Direct needs assessment in the library means not only inventorying and evaluating the effectiveness of current services but also soliciting input for planning purposes. To begin, information should be gathered from staff members who interact directly with students seeking homework assistance. What do the students request most? Do they want to learn to use the computers to conduct research to complete homework assignments, or do they want assistance navigating the stacks? Staff can report on patterns of homework help requested and offered and make suggestions to consider for planning your menu of homework help services.

It is also critical to find out from your clients—your customers—what they use and what they would like to see on your menu. Several options are available to help you approach your users:

Reference interviews. The same principles used to assess general satisfaction with library services can be applied to find out what works and what is needed for homework help. Plosker (2002) writes, "Librarians might ask additional questions at the conclusion of the traditional reference interview to see if key users have ideas on enhancing and extending user services. Do they, or would they, use online databases if remote access were provided? Would e-mail reference service be useful? What about chat technologies—would patrons use a chat function to communicate with professional reference staff remotely?"

Online surveys. Many libraries use a link to an online survey for patrons to evaluate their library services. Again, many of these surveys relate to overall library use, but librarians can tailor them to determine homework help needs. A link can be created for the children's, teens', and homework library web pages so customers can let you know what they like and what they would like to see regarding assistance with their homework.

Hard copy surveys. Opportunities abound to encourage young patrons to fill out a survey to help you plan homework help. Librarians can distribute surveys to young patrons as they use library facilities and distribute the surveys at events such as poetry slams, book club discussions, gaming nights, and other programs or activities for children and young adults.

Teen advisory groups. According to Lisa Matte, teen services librarian at the Jervis Public Library in Rome, New York, using a teen advisory group improves services to children, teens, and adults and facilitates wiser use of funds and staff time. Involving your group in both your homework help needs assessment and planning processes is one way it can do this.[1]

Parents. Although some students are old enough to drive themselves or take public transportation to the library, many depend on their parents to bring them. Furthermore, for homeschooled children the library is an integral part of the education process. Interviews and surveys of parents can help librarians determine which facilities and services are most valuable to students as they complete their homework assignments.

Needs Assessment in the Schools

One major weakness of data collected in the library is that they can only address the concerns of existing patrons. Information from other sources, such as schools and community organizations, can provide insight into the needs of young patrons who may not yet utilize your services.

School districts are expert in collecting enrollment data, which indicate who is attending your local schools and, therefore, your potential homework help customers. At the very least, most districts collect data about age and grade level enrollment in their schools, which identify the numbers and proportion of homework help users for any given grade. More elaborate analyses might include enrollment data by gender, race, or economic circumstances, data that you can use to familiarize yourself with characteristics of your users' community. The curriculum at each grade level is also usually public record. Some districts post it online; others can make it available to you in hard copy on request.

In this era of standards-based education and No Child Left Behind, most school districts also collect and publish standardized test results. The results drive curriculum development in many school buildings and districts as educators scramble to meet state and national requirements. Examining the general trends in standardized test results in your local school districts can give you some insight into the areas of weakness likely to be addressed in your community. For example, if you live in a community where most students passed the tenth-grade English exam administered by the state but performance on the Algebra I exam was unsatisfactory, you can anticipate that the school will emphasize algebra instruction. In turn, students may get more algebra homework, and you can anticipate more requests in the library for help with algebra assignments.

For direct needs assessment, arrange to visit the schools within your district for the specific purpose of assessing homework help needs. Cooperation between schools and libraries has not always been optimum, which has affected librarians' ability to help students complete homework, but for the past twenty years this situation has been changing. Take advantage of any existing cooperative relationships between local schools and your library, or foster your own relationships. Consult with school administrators and teachers about their priorities and ways they feel the library facilities and staff can support their students' learning process. See if it is possible to discuss specific needs with grade team leaders so you can be familiar with the timing and nature of instructional units for which you can provide student support outside the school building. Some schools have their own formal homework help programs, and a discussion with the coordinator of such programs may help you assess what additional student homework assistance can be provided at the library.

School librarians or media specialists are among your best resources in local schools. The roles of the youth librarian at a public library and the school librarian are quite different, as noted earlier. However, school librarians *can* enlighten you about the information needs of the students they instruct and may even be able to work with you to develop collection goals that complement the school library's holdings.

Through the school, you should be able to access the PTA, PTO, or similar organization with whom you can work to assess the homework help needs in your community. You might consider asking to speak at a PTA meeting to solicit input for developing your homework help program, or you might ask if you can post a request for feedback about homework help on the PTA electronic discussion list if one exists, and increasingly they do. If you address the PTA, you can also request that members speak to their children about completing user surveys for the purposes of planning homework help.

Needs Assessment in the Community

Collecting data from the community at large is important to a homework program needs assessment because the services in your program should reflect the characteristics of your constituency. For example, service to a community with a large Latino or African American population might include more computers, since these groups are far less likely to have home Internet access than their white and Asian counterparts, even though the vast majority of school districts have teachers who assign homework assignments requiring Internet use (ALA 2009b). Similarly, if your community has a large proportion of nonnative speakers, then ESL courses or bilingual online or in-house tutoring might be an important feature of your homework help menu of services. A good deal of this information is available through local, state, and federal data, such as the U.S. Census. As Connor (1990, 103) advocates, librarians should learn "as much as possible about the service area and what is available for children there. This helps focus on community needs that the library may be able to meet."

In addition, community needs assessment can and should be an ongoing process. Pierce County (Washington) Library System youth services coordinator Judy Nelson "took to heart what another children's librarian once told her: 'Be at the table. When the community is meeting or discussing anything, be there, wearing a name tag that says you are from the library'" (Library Journal 2005). Not only does this get the message across that the library is part of the community and a resource for it, but it enables you to gain a firsthand, albeit anecdotal, understanding of the concerns of the community you serve.

Direct needs assessment for large-scale library projects or extensive change to the library as a whole involves stakeholder interviews and focus groups. Although the development of a homework help program may not require hiring consultants or conducting multiple meetings, if you invite community members to express their priorities to you about your homework help program, you can use their ideas and support for both planning and funding purposes.

SURVEY THE EXISTING LIBRARY RESOURCES

Homework help, like every other program in the library, requires resources: people to run it, money to operate it, and supplies for patrons to use. While the needs assessment is being completed, it is also important to survey the resources already available for the implementation of the new program. Until you are certain of the specific needs in your community and the types of programs your library is willing to implement to meet those needs, it is not especially useful to begin the budgeting process. Librarians do, however, need to know up front what current options exist to equip a new program. Considerations include the following:

Funding. Has the library governing board or director already earmarked funds for a homework program? Even if this is not the case, has any funding been earmarked for specific technology that would be useful in a homework help program, such as additional computers in the building or new reference software? If so, youth librarians can make an effective argument to allocate the funding fully or partially to the homework help program. Also, it is important to begin the process of identifying potential outside sources of funding, since this may affect which options you can offer your patrons once you determine their needs. The 1997 LSTA is still the major federal grant program for libraries, and your state or county may have established financial resources for specific kinds of library programs. Some funding sources are available only for a limited timeframe, and if you imagine beginning the program with such grant allocations it is important to examine other opportunities for funding once the initial source dries up.

Space. Does your library building have any underutilized space that can be rearranged to become a homework help area? Will you have to integrate homework help onto the library floor, and if so can you obtain consent to rearrange stacks and furniture to set aside a corner for your program? Walter and Meyers (2003, 61–62) suggest looking to areas in your building where usage patterns have changed to find space. For example, if your library used to have a large area to house periodicals, that large area may not experience heavy usage because so many periodicals are now posted online.

Furniture and supplies. One way to determine whether your library has "extra" furniture for use in a homework help zone is to do walk-throughs yourself. Are patrons spread out one or two people per table large enough for six or eight, or are the reading tables jammed most of the time? Does your building have a storage closet filled with unused furniture, and if so is that furniture likely to be useful in a homework area or is it drab and dreary? Similarly, scrutinize available supplies—pens, paper, paper clips, staples. Does your library seem to have plenty available, or is the staff always scrounging for a paper clip? Even if your library has ample supplies, you cannot necessarily infer that plenty will be available for a homework help program's use, but it does indicate that administrators recognize the need to keep office supplies available.

People. Who will likely be assigned to plan and implement a homework help program? Will the work be split among several librarians and staff members who have sufficient available time to participate in the project without impinging on current duties, or will you need to hire more people? Does your library have an organized group of volunteers to whom you can go for help with various aspects of the program, such as supervising a study area set up in a conference room?

Technology. How many computers and copy machines are available in your library? Are they dedicated to one group of users or another (e.g., only adults or only students between certain hours) part or full time? How heavily are they used? How do you anticipate having to supplement the technology you have available now?

Local/state consortia. Is your library a member of a consortium? If so, does the consortium offer benefits such as librarian-staffed reference services shared among member libraries? Does your library participate in this? What steps would you have to take to become part of the consortium's group reference service. If your library is not a member of a consortium but one is available, would membership allow you to offer better or more homework help services, such as user access to a homework hotline vendor (e.g., Tutor.com or Brainfuse)? If the answer is yes, investigate the steps necessary to join the consortium. Also, look into what assistance your state offers the library; many offer statewide access to databases or online homework tutors.

The resources you finally end up employing in your range of homework help services may not resemble the list you compile when you survey what you have to start with, but you won't know what you need to ask for until you know what you already have at your disposal.

DELINEATE SPECIFIC GOALS

The role of the public library associated with providing homework help is to serve as a "formal education support center," a broad aim that drives the more specific goal setting required to plan a specific program or range of programs.

For a specific program, you need to consider the end you want to achieve and the specific tasks that must be completed to reach that end. This involves identifying general goals the library wants to fulfill and then specific, measurable outputs that will be used to achieve each goal. Table 1 illustrates how a specific program or activity can help achieve a broader goal.

Here are some of the areas librarians might consider addressing when they formulate homework help goals:

+ Information literacy
+ Culturally sensitive instruction
+ Access to technology
+ Access to hard copy and digital reference materials
+ Research skills and results
+ General study skills
+ Completion of daily school assignments
+ Academic achievement
+ Reference services
+ Safe afterschool environment

The programs you select to implement and the methods you employ to evaluate them will vary depending on the specific goals you set. For example, to help increase students' daily assignment completion rate, your library might implement a "homework alert" program (see below) and then measure the number of homework alerts received as part of your evaluation process. A more detailed description of possible measures and the evaluation process for your program is discussed in chapter 9.

DETERMINE YOUR PHILOSOPHY

A philosophy assessment is just as important as a needs assessment. The needs you assess belong to your patrons and surrounding community. The philosophy you assess is the vision you have for your library. Patrons, their teachers, the community, and the data may create one view of the ideal homework help program that you would establish if you had no budgetary, staff, or space limitations, but this is the real world, and you have logistical and financial limitations. You and your staff need to give some thought to the general approach you want to take as you develop your homework help menu of options. At the heart of the matter is whether you will provide formal homework help, a menu of information possibilities, or a combination of the two.

Formal Homework Programs

Mediavilla makes strong arguments for implementing formal homework centers to solve several problems, such as an ALA forecast that the need for homework-related library services will increase in the coming years and that there will be large numbers of unattended students in libraries across the nation. She writes that by "instituting formal after-school programs, librarians find that they can more readily focus their young patrons' energies on short-term project, such as completing their homework" (2001, 2–3), and outlines benefits of homework centers, such as increased self-esteem and improved socialization for participants.

Formal homework programs require a commitment of time, effort, and money. Librarians must pay staff or recruit qualified volunteers to provide tutoring, train tutors, coordinate and supervise tutors, and find an appropriate space in the library to dedicate to the program. These resources are not always available. Also, formal homework programs require students to be in the library building or another designated site during specific hours. This may not be possible for all of the patrons who want homework assistance. The athlete described in the preface, for example, will often find the library doors locked by the time she arrives at the building; she will most benefit from a program she can access from a remote location.

Finding qualified tutors may be a challenge, though at least one large library system partnered with educators to create a program with qualified tutors. The Chicago Public Library's drop-in "Teacher in the Library" program for elementary school students, staffed by paid, accredited teachers, provides formal homework help and answers parents' questions about helping their children complete assignments. The program runs two to four days per week, two to three hours per day, depending on the branch. Other libraries run their homework centers under the auspices of their literacy staff, or they contract the service out. Typically, however, volunteers are recruited for the purpose of staffing the homework help programs.

Not all library homework centers are within the library walls. Judy Nelson began bringing library services to her low-income income patrons and to those living in areas with low test scores. Her "Explorer Bookmobile," expandable to permit her to host an entire class, is equipped with two computer stations and serves as the backdrop for a portable homework help program (Library Journal 2005).

If the librarians in your branch or system are committed to starting and operating exactly this type of formal homework program, then detailed

TABLE 1

Sample Public Library Goals and Homework Help Objectives Designed to Achieve Them

LIBRARY SYSTEM/STATE	GOAL	OBJECTIVE TO ACHIEVE THE GOAL
Dayton Metro Public Library (Ohio)[a]	Traditional and nontraditional students and teachers will find resources, programs, services, and staff to support their educational endeavors.	By 2010, 6,000 hours of onsite or online homework help assistance will be provided to students at or through the library.
Fresno County Public Library (California)[b]	County residents, pre-K through adult, who are in formal learning programs will use materials and resources in relevant formats to support their academic goals.	Use of electronic databases and library homework help web pages will increase by 8% each year.
Greenlee Public Library System (Arizona)[c]	Collaborate with school districts and homeschool teachers to improve communication between school, homeschooled students, and libraries.	Request information annually from area teachers on student projects. Activity: Send out questionnaire at beginning of school year.
Le Mars Public Library (Iowa)[d]	Flexibility in planning, remaining proactive in developing outreach services, and expanding in-house program ideas are essential ingredients to children's services success.	Examine afterschool programs (reading, homework help, etc.) with children's librarian and using volunteers by September 2007.
Lewiston Public Library (Maine)[e]	Connect to the online world.	Conduct annual at least one series of website development classes targeted at either children or teens.
Shelter Rock Public Library (New York)[f]	Students in the Shelter Rock community will benefit from a stronger connection between the library and the school districts that serve them.	Create and promote an assignment notification link on the library's web page for use by teachers.

Sun Prairie Public Library (Wisconsin)[g]	The Sun Prairie Public Library will provide a broad range of programs, materials, and services to meet the needs of the community for information, ongoing educational opportunities, and the desire for personal growth and development.	Each year the Sun Prairie Public Library staff will help the public find answers to at least 75–80% of reference questions asked in person, by telephone, or e-mail. Representative activity: Promote Homework Help service on the library website, in schools, and through other organizations that support school-age children.
Tigard Public Library (Oregon)[h]	Youth in Tigard will have ready access to materials and information in a variety of formats that will allow them to develop basic research skills, complete homework assignments, and meet their broader information needs.	Develop and implement a "Homework Help" page on the Library's website (2007); at least 75% of youth surveyed will indicate that they received or had access to the information they needed to complete their homework assignments (Dec. 2008).
Tiverton Library Services (Rhode Island)[i]	Improve outreach to school-age children in elementary grades.	Provide outreach to homeschool families, providing an educational link and resources.

[a]Dayton Metro Library. 2008. Turning your ideas into reality: The Dayton Metro Library's 2008 strategic plan for results: Process, activities, and program opportunities, 19. www.daytonmetrolibrary.org/docs/PlanStrategic2008.pdf.

[b]Fresno County Public Library. 2004. Long range goals and objectives 2004–2006, 5. www.fresnolibrary.org/about/lrp0406.pdf.

[c]Greenlee County Library System Strategic Plan, 2004–2009, 6. www.lib.az.us/extension/GreenleeCounty.pdf (discontinued).

[d]Le Mars Public Library. Plan of service: Long range plan for Le Mars Public Library, 2006–2009. www.lemars.lib.ia.us/about/lrp2.

[e]Lewiston Public Library. Five-year-plan: 2009–2013, 5. http://lplonline.org/wp-content/uploads/long-range-plan-2009_1.pdf.

[f]Shelter Rock Public Library Board of Trustees. 2006. Long range plan 2006-2010. http://nassaulibrary.com/shelterrock/SRPL%20Long%20Range%20Plan%202006-2010.htm.

[g]Sun Prairie Public Library Board of Trustees. 2006. Sun Prairie Public Library plan of service 2006 (3–5 years), 5. www.sunprairiepubliclibrary.org/PlanofService.pdf.

[h]Tigard Library Board. 2005. Strategic plan 2005–2010: Mapping the future. www.tigard-or.gov/library/about/docs/library_strategic_plan.pdf.

[i]Tiverton Library Services. 2008. Long range plan 2008–2013, 2. www.tivertonlibrary.org/LongRangePlan2008-2013.pdf.

instructions for designing and implementing one can be found in Mediavilla's text (2001) .

Informal Homework Options

If a formal homework center is not feasible in your library because of staff, budget, or space constraints, or because you and your administration are not convinced it best meets the homework help needs in your community, there are many other options to provide assistance to students with their assignments. Formal online, telephone, chat, and e-mail tutoring and reference services are discussed in chapter 5. Several additional options for providing informal homework in the library are as follows:

Maintain a homework resource collection. Include reference books, copies of homework assignments that students bring with them, and a few basic school supplies such as a rulers, calculators, pens, and paper. If you locate the homework resource collection in a central spot, it gives students a designated place to congregate to do their homework (Sullivan 2005, 85–86).

Maintain binders of homework assignments from nearby schools. If you can establish a good working relationship with teachers and administrators at your local schools, you may be able to arrange to receive assignments in advance, which would be ideal. If this is not possible, staff members can still ask to copy an assignment for a binder when a student asks for assistance. Sources of information and assistance for the assignment can be noted on the back so the youth librarian or other staff members do not have to reinvent the wheel when another student arrives with the same assignment or when the teacher assigns the same project or problems the following year.

Keep as many of the textbooks used in your local schools as you can afford. Many libraries, such as the Public Library of Union County in Lewisberg, Pennsylvania, maintain copies of textbooks in their reference sections. Reference librarian Linda Homa reports, "Students who have forgotten a book can come to the library to use it. Some students regularly copy the pages for their assignments so they don't have to carry their books. Home school parents use them as well" (AASL/ALSC/YALSA 2004).

Reserve computers—the more the merrier—for student use during specific hours after school. Be prepared to provide information literacy instruction on how to use the computers most effectively for information and data base searches. Computer technology and information literacy instruction are discussed further in chapter 4.

Provide separate study areas for students to use after school. See "Location, Location, Location," below.

Provide traditional face-to-face reference services informed by pedagogical research and proven method. Student information-seeking behavior, the nature of homework reference queries, and how best to respond to students given current pedagogical theory and best practices are discussed in chapter 6.

Budgetary and space constraints aside, the choice between creating a homework center and focusing your homework help menu on informal assistance is philosophical. A homework center trumpets the new role of the library as a formal component of the education process. An informal menu of homework help services tends to reflect the more traditional view of the library as a place students can go voluntarily for supplementary assistance and support. Either perspective requires sound and thorough planning to ensure success.

Another philosophical question librarians must consider is how much of the homework assistance your library provides will take place in the building itself, through strategies listed above and face-to-face reference encounters, and how much will take place from remote locations. Chapter 5 includes a more detailed discussion of library websites and remote reference services such as telephone, e-mail, and chat reference services.

LOCATION, LOCATION, LOCATION

The space in the library where homework help services are dispensed may be almost as important as the nature of the services you provide. Walter and Meyers (2003, 58) point out that "the early architects of teen services . . . understood that place was essential for service," and Mediavilla concurs: "The space itself . . . gives kids a sense of place where they can make homework a priority" (2001, 33). Most libraries recognize that young patrons need a space in which to study off the library floor and provide study spaces for young adults, children, or both.

When you home in on a space in the library for homework help and studying, you may have limited options, but to the extent possible selection should be made with sensitivity to your patrons' concerns. One important consideration is the distinction between young adults and children. Younger students may look up to older students, but sometimes they are also intimidated by them. The antipathy is not one-sided, either. As lovely and inviting as the children's section of your library may be, teenagers will probably blanch at the prospect of going there for homework help, and some of them, perhaps all of them, may refuse to utilize the service if that is the only space available for it. In fact, teenagers generally prefer their space to be as far as possible from the children's section of the library (Vaillancourt 2000). If it is feasible given your facilities, children and young adults study spaces should be located in separate areas.

Once you locate space for your program, the challenge of designing it and making it functional lies ahead of you. One of your best resources for effective planning in this area is to engage your staff and teen advisory group or other patron representatives at every stage of this process. They are the experts in what appeals to young patrons, so the success of your homework help services is more assured if they help plan it. Bring your ideas about floor plans and equipment to them, and solicit their advice.

As you plan, keep in mind certain factors that can affect how inviting and useful the space will be to your users—the same factors that impact all youth services facilities: noise level, lighting, furniture, technology. Traditionally, parents have always been advised to find quiet places for the children to study, which suggests that they need quiet places to study in the library, too. On the other hand, modern pedagogy emphasizes collaborative learning, and the increasing number of cooperative homework projects means that you also need to provide areas where students can gather to discuss their assignments. If your budget allows, you should install full-spectrum lighting, which has the properties of natural sunlight. Studies have found that using full spectrum lighting correlates with school children's academic success (Feinberg et al. 1998). Proximity to the curriculum-related collections and school supplies is also desirable. Convenience counts. Safety and supervision are important factors for both children and young adults, especially if students are in a more isolated area off the main library floor. Can a staff member be spared to work in the assigned location? If not, can the program be moved to a space that is visible from the librarian's desk? These are basic questions of safety for your patrons. You may not have the budget available to do a full room makeover, but the more you design your space based on your patrons' preferences, the more inviting your space will be. Parents of teenagers, for example, frequently see their offspring prefer sofas and easy chairs to tables and desks, even though this demands extra agility to balance computers, textbooks, and notebooks on their knees. For children and young adults, practicality is important, but comfort is significant, too.

Even though we are full throttle into the age of Facebook, texting, IM-ing, and other electronic information social networking, the first thing your users see when they enter the library is what you put on your walls. Signs and bulletin boards still make a difference. They should be visually appealing. Also, your patrons' entire perspective on the library can be defined by the way you word posted instructions. Jones and Shoemaker (2001, 42–43) provide the following illustrative example: "Consider the difference between a sign that says 'STOP! No students beyond this point!!!!' vs. a kinder, gentler one that says 'Staff work area: please ask staff before using this area.'"

COORDINATING WITH YOUR
LOCAL SCHOOL SYSTEMS

In the best of all possible homework help worlds, libraries are fully informed about their local schools' curricula and teachers' specific assignments in advance of the onslaught of students seeking help with those assignments. Alas, this is not the best of all possible worlds. Still, librarians can employ several strategies to improve library-school coordination.

Know the Curriculum

Collecting and becoming acquainted with the curricula across all grade levels, or delegating specific grade levels to various staff members, helps you provide more knowledgeable and useful assistance to students. You can tailor your collections accordingly and separate out literature relevant to specific school units for each grade. This literature can be displayed or housed in the homework help area. Familiarity with the curricula has another advantage: it helps promote more constructive relationships with school administrators, teachers, and media specialists. You will speak the same language.

As noted earlier, curricula are usually public information. Also, the school librarian or media specialist can help keep you updated with anticipated changes in curricula. Typically, school administrators and teaching staff meet toward the end of the school year to decide the approaches they will take for the next school year, and they meet at the beginning of the school year to share strategies to teach the material. The school librarian or media specialist is usually included in or informed about this process and may be willing to forward curriculum changes to a school liaison on your staff who can ensure the information reaches the appropriate coordinator of your children's or young adult's homework help program. Alternatively, you can contact grade team leaders in elementary schools or department heads in middle and high schools to find out anticipated changes to their curricula from year to year, as well as to reiterate the support the library can provide their students.

Use Homework Alerts

Post a homework alert form on your library's website if you have one; if not, distribute a stack of hard-copy homework alert forms to the school and arrange to retrieve them. A homework alert is a means through which teachers in your community schools can notify you in advance about assignments that they anticipate will result in students visiting the library for additional information. The simplest forms might involve a brief space in which the teacher describes an assignment; more complex forms might break down the assignment into various components, requirements, and special instructions. Below is a list of fields that might be included on a library homework alert form. The list is neither prescriptive nor exhaustive; it is intended to give you options you can use to get started. Those items that should appear on every form are indicated by an asterisk.

+ School*
+ Branch(es) to which students will go to complete the assignment
+ Teacher's name and contact information (E-mail is preferable, since many teachers are unable to speak on the phone for most of their work day because they are in class, and often many teachers share one telephone number.)*
+ Grade level for the assignment*
+ Course title (if appropriate)*
+ Assignment topic
+ Number of students or classes receiving the assignment*
+ Start date/due date*
+ Required materials
+ Excluded materials
+ Brief description of the assignment. Suggest to teachers that they can cut and paste the assignment in the space provided if possible; this shortens the time they have to spend on the form.*
+ Box to check if the assignment is annual
+ Request to set aside materials for students to use in the library
+ Request to receive a bibliography or other materials relevant to the assignment via e-mail
+ Contact at the library to whom teachers can speak if they have a question about the form or assignment

Don't be surprised if teachers are not as enthusiastic as you are about the idea of homework alerts. On the one hand, most teachers welcome support from the library for their instruction. On the other hand, they may feel that filling out the form for each major assignment is yet one more detail they need to take care of among the ever-growing administrivia on their plates. Any ideas to shorten the amount of time and effort required to fill out the form will win more cooperation from teachers. One such idea is to provide boxes to click next to various sources that should be included or excluded from the assignment (e.g., periodicals, websites, books, encyclopedias) instead of asking teachers to type in which kinds of materials apply. Another thoughtful touch is to provide a place on the form where teachers can request specific kinds of support from you, such as biographies or subject guides. If the e-mail format for public school teachers in all of your districts is the same, fill in the portion of the e-mail address common to all staff to further cut the time teachers need to spend filling out the form. Finally, keep in mind that the shorter the form the better, from the teacher's perspective. It may be tempting to ask for an elaborate breakdown of the assignment, a list of resources the teacher has already provided to the students, or details about the assignment. Or you may want to use the opportunity to ask for additional information for your own purposes even though it is only peripherally related to the assignment (e.g., how the teacher heard about the homework alert program). Remember: the more information you request, the less likely teachers will happily use the form more than a couple of times.

Assign a Liaison to the Local Public and Private Schools

If your library already has an individual or group that fosters cooperative programs between the schools and libraries, take advantage of that connection to advocate a system of communication that supports an effective homework program, such as homework alerts. This is also a perfect opportunity to solicit educators' input into how you can best organize your homework help menu of services to meet the needs of their students. If your library does not have a liaison, the youth librarian should do this or assign someone to make contacts at local schools. When Fitzgibbons (2000) reviewed the research available on cooperative programs between schools and public libraries, she found that communication was the most important factor in cooperation.

Larger organizations often facilitate communication between schools and libraries in larger school districts. For example, the three systems in New York City participate in the Connecting Libraries and Schools Project, a joint school-library organization that establishes a range of programs depending on the needs of communities served by particular libraries. Similarly, in Fairfield, Ohio, the Partners in Education project focused on the ways school library media specialists and public librarians could work together to communicate school assignments and provide access to needed materials: "The most important ingredient identified was the development of open channels of communication, both formal (such as teacher newsletters, in-person contacts, and records of annual assignments) and informal (such as social occasions and face-to-face meetings)" (Fitzgibbons 2000).

Establishing direct contacts with the school may also make school personnel more responsive to allowing you to put announcements in the school newsletter to let staff, parents, and students know about homework help resources at the library or to request their input into your program's planning process.

Develop an Ongoing Relationship with School Librarians

Some schools do not have a librarian or media specialist in their buildings, but most do. The school librarian is a valuable resource for cooperative planning for homework help in the library. Each of you has information or materials that can help the other do her job more effectively. You can provide information, lend material to the school library to supplement its collection, and provide assistance to students after the school building has closed; the school librarian knows the curricula, staff expectations from students, and what kinds of information literacy skills prove challenging to students in the building. Either the librarian or a liaison should start the process with visits to the school library and meetings to establish shared goals and complementary resources. One option to nurture sensitivity to the similarities and differences in your respective roles is to conduct your own reality show experiment for a few days. The media specialist and a public librarian in Lexington, Massachusetts, in fact, exchanged jobs for a full year with the support of their respective oversight organizations (Fitzgibbons 2000).

Circulate a Newsletter to Local Teachers

A newsletter can serve the dual purpose of publicity and opening lines of communication to bolster school-library cooperation. For example, the Mid-Hudson Library System in New York and the Multnomah (Oregon) County Library publish quarterly newsletters to publicize new programs, describe resources that can assist teachers, and announce upcoming events. Newsletters can also be used to solicit input into the homework help planning process and cooperation for homework alert programs. Depending on your budget and the cooperation of school administrators, you may be able to distribute a copy of the newsletter to every teacher via their mailboxes at school or ask that the newsletter be posted for teachers in the appropriate location at school. Another option is to publish an e-mail newsletter to distribute to teachers, but if you do this figure out a way to highlight information in the subject line and first sentence so the teachers are encouraged to open and read the e-mail.

YOUR STAFF: KEEP THEM IN THE LOOP AND TRAIN THEM

A major resource for planning a homework help program is right in your library: your staff. It is especially important to get staff on board early in the planning process, since they will likely be on the front lines of implementing your program. If they are not enthusiastic about providing homework help in the programs you establish, kids will detect this and be ambivalent about your services. Changes in any organization are met with varying degrees of resistance, but involving staff at the start minimizes that resistance and improves the quality of your program. Approaching staff only at the implementation stage will, at best, cause resentment and, at worst, deny you the opportunity to include the expertise your staff can contribute to the planning process. In his discussion of successfully implementing social software in libraries, Stephens (2006) recommends putting together a team with representatives from every part of your library organization and begins his list of ten steps for "achieving staff buy-in" with "Listen to your staff." In the planning stages, librarians should convene meetings with the staff who will be affected by a new homework help service to discuss their ideas and solicit their feedback on information collected from users and school and community representatives.

Advances in technology have also improved the range of options you have for soliciting ideas from staff and sharing information, such as budgets, objectives, and progress reports, with them: "Staff wikis scream to be used to develop plans and timelines for all staff to access and review" (Stephens 2006).

Training staff effectively is equally important. How can staff support the approach of your program if they don't know how to incorporate it into their jobs? Both formal training, such as the elements discussed in chapter 3, and informal support for incorporating new ideas and technologies into the library homework help services will prove important to the success of the program.

✳   ✳   ✳

The planning process for designing your homework help menu of services is complex. You must assess what your patrons need and want by taking into consideration a wide range of factors, from the demographics of your community to what makes for a comfortable workspace for young patrons. Resources you already have at your disposal should be reviewed, and potential outside sources for funding should be identified. Staff should be involved in the planning process from the outset, as should your young patrons themselves via informal discussions, focus groups, or teen advisory groups. Coordination with local schools is an integral part of a successful homework program because it enables you to learn the nature of your young patrons' assignments and tailor your reference materials and services to them. You also need to determine the philosophical approach librarians in your building want to take to homework assistance; will you provide formal tutoring, a range of informal homework help services, or both? To figure out the best approach to take and to implement that approach, you need the input and cooperation of one of the library's greatest resources: your staff. Once you bring them on board with the homework help program planning and determine what to include in your menu of services, it is your frontline staff who will be responsible for implementing many aspects of the program.

Note

1. For a detailed description of how and why to set up a TAG and types of projects for the group, see Matte's online pamphlet, "A Teen Advisory Group: What's in It for My Library?" at www.jervislibrary.org/YAWeb/NYLAps_TAG.pdf.

THREE

Staff Training and Professional Development

M ANY EXPERTS ADDRESS principles of staff training in general and library staff training in particular. All of these experts agree with the ALA philosophy that "continuous learning is critical to renewing the expertise and skills needed to assist patrons in this information age. Library workers must continually expand their knowledge in order to keep up with the rate of change . . . whether you are an entry-level professional, mid-career librarian, support staff, senior management staff or trustee" (ALA 2009a). Like managers of all programs in the library, those youth services librarians who oversee homework help programs must consider the training necessary to start the program or initiate changes to it as well as to enhance staff skill sets to keep up with the times.

To create an effective training program for homework help, the approach that drives your homework help services must be clearly established, the role the staff will play in providing homework help must be determined, and you must choose the methods to be used to provide the training.

HOMEWORK HELP APPROACH

Chapter 2 includes a discussion of the import of conducting a philosophy assessment to decide whether to provide formal or informal homework help or both to students. Staff training varies to some degree depending on the nature of the program. If your library offers primarily formal programs in which volunteers work one-on-one with students during certain afterschool hours, then this will inform your staff training; they must know how to work with or supervise groups of volunteers and participate in the process of preparing the library for the formal program implementation on a regular basis. If your staff is primarily expected to help support more informal homework assistance, from responding to reference queries to helping students navigate a homework resource collection, then a different set of skills should be emphasized in staff training.

A basic understanding of youth and teen development is useful to any staff member who will interact with students. Libraries are very likely to serve diverse populations, and to ensure that all students feel welcome in your library and on your library web pages your training program should include a portion devoted to cultural diversity sensitivity and the cultural standards important to the populations served in your community. Adopting the customer service model requires familiarizing your staff with basic customer service principles. Similarly, implementing the concept of the library as a gathering place, both face-to-face and in the virtual world, requires an understanding of "the four Cs" and how to foster each of them: conversation, connections, community, and collaboration.

The staff's facility with new information technology is fundamental to the success of your homework help program, and therefore training in these tools should be at the core of your training program. Information and communication technologies are changing so rapidly that what was current just a few years or even months ago is no longer relevant, but they are such important aspects of homework assistance that the frequency of training staff in technology should be ongoing.

YOUR STAFF'S ROLE IN HOMEWORK SUPPORT

To determine what kinds of training will be most valuable with precious dollars and time available, first you must determine the specific roles your professional and support staff will be expected to play in the homework help program.

Only then can you establish the precise skills they need to learn and how the training should proceed.

Some roles will be identical to those they play anywhere else in the library. For example, staff will help students locate materials to complete homework assignments, just as they help adults find materials they need for business or personal purposes. However, some roles are specific to providing homework help. The key to deciding which roles your staff will play is to include them in the process. The people on the front lines of your youth services program are in a unique position to observe students' needs, and their perspective may lead them to think of creative and realistic ways to meet those needs.

A list of the roles you and your staff should consider adopting for a homework help program follows. Each role requires training tailored to the services involved.

+ Should staff be volunteer coordinators who oversee a one-on-one homework help program several days a week? If so, how can you best facilitate this?
+ Should some nonlibrarian staff be assigned to provide directional assistance to students as they enter the youth services area, and, if so, how can this be appropriately arranged in your space to be clear to the patrons?
+ Will staff maintain subject guides?
+ Should subject areas be assigned to specific staff members to whom students can be referred for help in specific areas?
+ How should staff be involved with coordinating homework help services with local schools?
+ What records will be kept and how will staff accomplish this? Records should include those necessary for evaluating the program as well as binders that contain copies of assignments by grade and subject.
+ Will staff operate a reserve system of books for long-term assignments that bring many students to the library looking for the same information?
+ Will staff conduct separate information literacy classes for students?
+ If computers are to be set aside for students' use for homework, how will this be enforced and supervised?

Most youth services staff involved in a homework help program also play the role of "interpreter"—interpreter of assignments. Before students can attempt to complete an assignment, they must understand what questions the teacher is asking. Once a student shares an assignment with a librarian, the librarian should be able to interpret it, breaking it down or helping the student break it down into smaller pieces so the tasks are more manageable. In addition, most librarians and other staff working with students doing homework in the library are information literacy instructors who teach students on a one-on-one basis, whether or not the program also includes teaching information literacy classes for students.

SKILLS AND BASIC KNOWLEDGE
FOR HOMEWORK SUPPORT

Several professional associations for libraries in general and youth services in particular have created descriptions of competencies necessary to provide appropriate services, including ALSC's "Competencies for Librarians Serving Children in Public Libraries" (2009), YALSA's "Competencies for Librarians Serving Youth" (2010), and AASL's "Standards for the 21st-Century Learner" (2007). The ALSC and YALSA documents include knowledge of the technology students will likely use while doing homework, knowledge of the local curriculum, and ways to achieve relational excellence.

The Library and Technology Association (LITA) introduced *Core Technology Competencies for Libraries,* by Susan Thompson (2008), to help ensure that librarians are sufficiently facile with new information technologies to be able to incorporate the ever-emerging latest developments. The media mix students use to communicate with each other and their teachers about homework provides tools to facilitate completing homework assignments, as noted earlier, and sometimes students will be assigned specifically to include new technologies as they complete homework. For example, teachers may create blogs in which students must participate, or they may ask students to create web content to contribute to the class. Even students in elementary school may use presentation software for class assignments. To provide effective homework help, your staff must be trained in these technologies.

Some of your staff will be enthusiastic about learning and applying new technologies, while others may see them as riddled with glitches or simply intimidating. Whether you provide incentives to overcome these barriers or try to ameliorate these concerns with gentle persuasion, eventually all staff assisting students with homework must become skilled users of these tools so that they, in turn, can help their patrons compete effectively with their peers on the digital playing field.

Knowledge of the local curricula and coordination with schools cannot be emphasized enough as critical areas of competence for any staff member working with students. Each subject for the curriculum in each grade consists of extensive descriptions of goals, skills, processes, markers, and occasionally specific assignments. No staff member can master it all, but staff should have a general overview of how the school year progresses. For example, your district's science curriculum may involve creating a science fair project in grades four and seven, or a research paper on an animal species in grade eight. The math curriculum in grades three and four may involve mastery of the multiplication tables. The more aware your staff are of the progression in each subject area, the better prepared they are to provide help to students at different grade levels. If you can partner with your local schools so that you learn about regular and long-term individual and class projects, staff professional development can include reviewing the projects and various library formats that can help students complete their assignments, such as databases, solid websites, subject guides, and word processing, spreadsheet, and presentation software.

Without relational intelligence and sensitivity geared specifically to school-age children and teenagers, all the skills and knowledge your staff acquire through training will come to naught. If your patrons cannot approach your staff or hear what they have to say, the staff will not be able to help them with homework. For some, talking to children or teenagers is natural. Others require training to become comfortable with kids. As per RUSA (Reference and User Services Association) and YALSA "Guidelines for Library Services to Teens Ages 12–18," librarians who work with all youth age groups must learn to "provide [youth] . . . with courteous and professional customer service at every service point," which means being pleasant and positive, respecting privacy, and embracing the diversity of your user population (RUSA and YALSA 2008).

Providing services to youth doing homework in the library requires particular sensitivity to the potential ambivalence of the homework patrons. A student who seeks your advice about a new book to read after she finishes all the volumes in the Twilight series looks forward to your recommendations with relish. Students doing homework, on the other hand, are often responding to "imposed queries" and "often do not know or are not interested in the content of what they are asking, but only know that they have to have it" (RUSA and YALSA 2008). Such a student may seem like a difficult patron at first blush, when in fact he may simply be frustrated about having to do an assignment he doesn't like. Staff members trained to anticipate these kinds of problems and apply various relational strategies to turn the situation around are most effective at providing homework assistance.

SUGGESTIONS FOR TRAINING METHODS

The range of training approaches available for staff professional development related to homework help is quite broad. We were all kids once, and maybe we have kids, or we have nieces and nephews and we talk to kids every day in our work. So communication with them should be a breeze, right? Not really. Being able to talk to kids is not the same thing as being able to help them learn. If we are to help them learn, students need to feel librarians are accessible, and librarians need to be responsive to students' relational concerns. For some of us, as noted above, this is natural, but it is far too important a factor in the homework help process to leave to chance. Staff should be trained in how to fine-tune their professional demeanor with the young patron in mind. The single most important concern is teaching staff to cultivate a positive attitude. Virtually all pedagogical literature emphasizes how important this is for students to respond well to adults in any educational setting.

Before you can determine which training approach works best for you, you need to decide how much of the budget will be allocated to training. Training formats range from spending a great deal of money on engaging outside consultants and sending your staff to professional conferences to utilizing structures already in place. The following formats can be mixed and matched as your budget and staff schedule allow.

Departmental Meetings

Dedicating a few departmental meetings or portions of meetings to training incorporates the training into the existing organizational structure. This is an especially useful venue for asking staff members to share progress on specific projects in your homework help program or techniques they have found to be particularly successful. One option is to assign various staff members to make short presentations in which they describe techniques or resources they find especially useful. If each staff member contributes techniques and resources, you can ensure that every person contributes to the collective knowledge that informs your homework help program.

Training Sessions and Workshops

These are what most of us typically think of when we think of staff training. Professional consultants can be hired to familiarize staff with implementing specific types of programs. You can also ask librarians, teachers, or administrators from your local schools to speak on specific topics in homework support. Experts in the community, such as a local child psychologist, might be willing to share relevant information with your staff. As a matter of professionalism, such speakers should be paid an honorarium whenever possible. If your budget does not allow for payment, some speakers might be willing to donate their time. Other relatively inexpensive options include asking staff working on special projects relevant to the homework program to create longer training programs for the projects they oversee as opposed to shorter presentations for staff meetings. A staff member who oversees a formal homework help program can discuss the structure of the program, which students are the best candidates to refer for formal tutoring, and the administrative details of the program. Members of your library's IT staff can conduct training sessions about equipment and software that can be especially useful for students doing homework in the building. Possible topics for training sessions and workshops also include the following:

Introduction to homework help: your homework assistance menu of services; what students need and what you can reasonably be expected to provide; technology available in the library and online; the library web page, helpful websites, databases, and word processing and spreadsheet programs.

The library as place: how homework help fits into the big picture of the library; creating comfortable places for students to work; encouraging students to gather in the library; changing traditional rules to make the library more appealing as a "town plaza"; using blogs to create a sense of online community for young people.

Local curricula and resources for studies in subject areas: Divide this into grades, such as pre-K to second grade, third to fifth grade, and so on. As an example, staff can be familiarized with journals such as the *School Library Journal,* which reviews and describes educational series and materials that are relevant to typical school curricula and publishes *Curriculum Connections* for this purpose.

Youth culture: music, clothing, television, gaming, social networks, and slang. Because establishing rapport is so important to the homework help process and because making the learning process relevant to students' lives is such an effective instructional method, understanding youth culture is an important tool.

Youth development: emotional, intellectual, and physiological aspects at each stage of development and how these impact academic endeavors in and out of the library.

Interpreting and breaking down long-term assignments into chunks. Use specific assignments students have brought to your library in the past; coordinate with local school staff to determine teachers' expectations; include relevant study habits to suggest to patrons, such as calendaring each chunk.

Difficult young patrons: managing confrontational behavior toward you or other patrons—what to say, nonverbal cues, how to redirect students' energies, how to keep your cool, and when to get help.

Interacting with students: techniques for engaging young patrons to find out information about their homework, monitoring progress, effective uses of feedback and praise.

Cultural sensitivity training: specific cultural norms in the populations you serve.

Sexual orientation sensitivity training: making young gay, lesbian, bisexual, and transgender (GLBT) patrons feel welcome in your library and homework program.

Recognizing and responding to learning styles: various "intelligences"; approaches that work best with each of the VAKT styles (see chapter 1).

Information technology for homework help: helping young patrons navigate the library catalog, databases, software, and online services.

If you hire outside consultants, you can presume they will bring all the appropriate bells and whistles, but if the sessions are in house, design them with the fundamental pedagogical strategies described in chapter 6 in mind; they work as well with the adults on your staff as they do with students in the classroom. Your staff members have different learning styles, too, so visual, aural, and kinesthetic elements should be included in every workshop. As Seattle Public Library's training coordinator Mary Bucher Ross suggests in "Tips for Technology Training" (2002), " 'chunk' content into digestible units, . . . offer choices whenever possible, . . . give immediate real-work applications for whatever you are demonstrating, . . . asking questions is more effective than giving answers, . . . [and] check for understanding." Ross also suggests having your staff work in collaborative groups and monitoring progress by circulating throughout the room.

Roundtables

A roundtable discussion is especially compelling for sharing ideas among professionals engaged in similar tasks, such as members of your staff who are involved in various aspects of your homework help program. Unlike a presentation by a staff member, roundtables encourage more give-and-take in the meeting, so each member of the staff learns from the others in one sitting and can leave the roundtable armed with techniques that have been successful for other staff members. Roundtables about homework help that take place in conjunction with your teen or youth advisory group can help staff learn about the needs and concerns of young patrons from their own perspective. Similarly, if you can arrange regular roundtables with your staff and representatives from local schools, you create a forum for your staff to learn about how educators and librarians can work together to help students achieve their educational goals.

Desk Cards

Create desk cards that contain directions to which staff can refer as they implement homework help with students. For example, you can have a desk card for how to access a particular database or use the printer, one for how to "chunk" long-term assignments, or one that contains your district's rubric for writing a good high school essay. Most of this information can be stored in staff computers, but the advantage of desk cards is their portability; librarians and other staff can bring appropriate cards with them as they circulate among your young patrons.

Professional Organizations and Community Involvement

Separate from training funded and implemented by the library, encourage your staff members to join professional organizations and become involved in local community groups. This does not provide traditional training, but your staff will acquire skills when they join professional organizations such as AASL, ALSC, YALSA, or LITA. Also encourage staff to join ALA roundtables such as the Library Support Staff Interests Roundtable or the GLBT Roundtable. The participation is advantageous for your staff because of the professional connections they make and the increased familiarity with cutting-edge developments in their field. The advantages to the library are the same relationships and cutting-edge knowledge brought back to the library. Community involvement is similarly advantageous to both your staff and your library in that your staff participates in new endeavors and acquires new skills of use to the library.

Online Resources

Internet training resources for librarians abound. Some schools of information services offer full degree programs, and most offer courses for credit that are relevant to providing homework support, such as courses in resources for children and young adults, information needs of youth, and information literacy.

PROFESSIONAL ORGANIZATIONS OF
INTEREST TO HOMEWORK HELP STAFF

YALSA: www.ala.org/ala/mgrps/divs/yalsa/yalsa.cfm

AASL: www.ala.org/ala/mgrps/divs/aasl/index.cfm

LITA: www.ala.org/ala/mgrps/divs/lita/index.cfm

Library Support Staff Interests Round Table: www.ala.org/ala/mgrps/rts/lssirt/index.cfm

GLBT Round Table: www.ala.org/ala/mgrps/rts/glbtrt/index.cfm

Professional groups offer classes as well for youth services librarians. For example, at this writing YALSA's online course catalog includes courses such as "AIMing at Tweens: Advising, Involving, Motivating," "New Technologies and New Literacies for Teens," and "Pain in the Brain: Adolescent Development and Library Behavior," all of which suggest developing a base of knowledge that will enhance any young adult librarian's ability to address the homework needs of patrons. ALSC's Summer 2010 offerings include "Children with Disabilities in the Library," "Out of This World Youth Programming" (which addresses networking in the community, planning, and evaluation among other topics), and "Reading Instruction and Children's Books." AASL and RUSA also offer courses, many of which will enhance your staff's knowledge and skills relevant to the homework program in your library.

Several free online resources help librarians with children's services and homework help. The Idaho Commission for Libraries offers free online courses through its Supplemental Alternative Basic Library Education (SABLE) program. Though fairly simplistic and therefore not necessarily useful for everyone, this program includes some basic, self-monitored learning about working with children and young adults, including how to treat youths and how to provide homework support. Homework help is addressed in both the sections on working with children and the one on working with young adults. The Online Programming for All Libraries (OPAL), an international consortium, includes some courses relevant to children's services and homework help, too, and WebJunction offers coursework that occasionally addresses relevant topics.

A final and extremely useful free resource for online training is Library 2.0's 23 Things. Helene Blowers, the IT director at the Charlotte and Mecklenberg County (North Carolina) Public Library, developed a nine-week course for librarians to learn twenty-three technology tasks, ranging from setting up blogs and RSS feeds to locating podcasts. The course is posted online, where it is accessible to anyone who wishes to master these skills. Libraries across the country have used this website or adapted its content for staff training purposes. One of the biggest advantages of this program is that staff can work at their own pace or even learn the "23 things" in the comfort of their own homes.

✳   ✳   ✳

Without training, your staff will root about trying to figure out how best to help students who arrive at your doors with homework assignments, but they will be armed with methods and theories that no longer apply. Keeping them up to date and continuous learners is advantageous to the staff, to the library, and to your patrons.

Once you delineate the programs you will provide and you work with the staff to determine the roles they should play to support these programs, you can identify specific skills your staff needs to learn or hone to be successful homework supporters and arrange for them to acquire those skills. Staff training can be accomplished whether you have a large enough budget to engage the services of outside consultants and reimburse staff members for attendance at state or national conferences, or whether you have very limited funds and must depend on structures already in place, volunteer speakers, and free online courses. Relatively inexpensive options include dedicating a portion of staff

---

ONLINE CONTINUING EDUCATION RESOURCES

YALSA online course catalog: www.ala.org/ala/mgrps/divs/yalsa/onlinecourses/info.cfm

ALSC Online education: Current online course offerings: http://0-www.ala.org.sapl.sat.lib.tx.us/ala/mgrps/divs/alsc/edcareeers/profdevelopment/alscweb/

Idaho Commission for Libraries, SABLE: http://libraries.idaho.gov/page/sable

OPAL: Online Programming for All Libraries: www.opal-online.org

WebJunction course catalog: www.webjunction.org/catalog

Learning 2.0: 23 Things: http://plcmcl2-things.blogspot.com

meetings to training, conducting roundtable discussions to share ideas and coordinate with patrons and with schools, providing cards to keep on hand to remind staff about how to use certain technologies or approach homework assignments, and encouraging staff to join professional organizations. Online, you and your staff will find resources that can greatly enhance skill and knowledge. Accredited schools of information services, professional organizations, and local and state library systems offer relevant courses of varying length, substance, and cost, and Library 2.0's 23 Things provides hands-on learning about and practice with manipulating new media for educational purposes.

FOUR

Technology in the Library
for Homework Help

I F I MISS one of the president's speeches that my neighbors loved and I want to know if I agree with them, or I want to understand why my college-age children become teary-eyed when they talk about Christian the Lion's reunion with the men who raised him, I needn't worry; with a click of a mouse or the flick of a finger on the keypad, I can pull up a video of either event on YouTube. I can then forward the link to others via e-mail or post it on my Facebook page. YouTube, e-mail, and Facebook have blended so seamlessly into the communication technologies available today that I don't think twice about using them—and neither do your young patrons. Still, they have not been around for very long. YouTube, for example, first hit the Internet in 2005. In his description of the important technological events over the lifespan of what he calls the "digital native," Rainie (2009) notes that Tim Berners-Lee wrote the World Wide Web program in 1990, Wikipedia was created in 2001, the iPod came out in 2002, and the first podcast took place in 2004. The way we access and collect information is changing substantially year by year. The information services community has been concerned for years about the impact these changes will have on the library, even fearing library buildings would become obsolete altogether early into the twenty-first century.

Yet here we are in 2010 and libraries are going strong. Though some patron cohorts are relative newcomers to the library buildings—for example, Wall Street brokers who find themselves unemployed because of the stock market plunge in 2008 and 2009—children and young people continue to be one of the central groups of in-house users. And many of them go to the library for the same reason they did ten, twenty, and thirty years ago: no matter how many new tools we invent, kids still need help with their homework. The difference today is how libraries can and do provide that help.

A final note before the discussion about specific approaches to technology in the library begins: technological change can be gradual or sudden, but a tool is relevant and useful only until a more efficient, faster, or more portable tool is invented to replace it. At this writing, the information here is accurate, but each new technological advance will, at some point in the future, become obsolete. This does not mean that the underlying concepts will lose their relevance. For example, students will benefit from being able to create or retrieve images and modify them for homework assignments, but the technologies they use to do so will undoubtedly change over time.

THE LIBRARY AS PLACE

For decades patrons went to the library primarily if not exclusively to meet their information needs. Whether they were motivated by recreational, business, or educational interests, the library was the place they could find books and information—for many, the *only* place they could access books and information. Now the situation is quite different. Information is everywhere, accessed in many different ways. Partly in response to this change, in the 1990s and 2000s a new paradigm for the library emerged: the concept of the library as a destination in and of itself, a community hub that hosts a range of activities from socializing to studying, gaming nights to discussion groups. This is *library as place*. The majority of the research related to library as place has taken place where it has been most comprehensively implemented: in academic libraries affiliated with universities and colleges. However, public and school libraries have begun to plan for library as space as well. In the latter part of the twentieth century, many noted the lack of places where the community could gather, such as the old-fashioned town center or village square. Oshkosh (Wisconsin) Public Library director John Nichols commented that "because that sense of 'place' in the community has really changed in America, the public library, especially in rural communities, is where people increasingly get together, whether it's for poetry, a concert, or a book reading. . . .

Opportunities to connect with people in person are getting fewer and fewer" (quoted in St. Lifer 2001). Just as architects have designed planned suburban communities that take this need for places to gather into account (e.g., Reston, Virginia, and Columbia, Maryland), others are beginning to design libraries as a place where the community can come together. Library as place serves a different purpose in an academic environment, where it provides "a one-stop shopping (learning) experience" (Freeman 2005). The idea is that students can access information or e-mail, use print collections, study, get help from the writing center, converse with their classmates, or engage in any number of other learning activities, all under one roof.

Although most of the literature about library as place relates to global planning for an entire library facility, the idea of a "one-stop shopping experience" for students who come to the library to do their homework has enormous potential. Two specific concepts that can be applied to homework help are the learning commons and the technology center. Both involve the centralization of information technology, among other services.

The Learning Commons

Many academic libraries have reorganized their reference services around a "learning commons." An information desk is set up in a centralized location where students gather and study. Students go to the information desk to ask for assistance, and the staff at the information desk determine their needs and send them to other areas in the library where they receive the appropriate help, whether in the writing center, in the advising office, or at a tech support desk or reference services area. As Jennifer McCabe, assistant director of the East Campus Library at James Madison University, writes, "We envision a space where our users will receive assistance with all activities related to scholarship under one roof" (McCabe 2007). Because they are so closely related to modern academic pursuits, information technology and instruction in how to utilize it are integral parts of the learning commons models.

Some K–12 school libraries have begun incorporating learning commons concepts, specifically the core feature of combining diverse services in one location. At Chelmsford High School in Massachusetts, library teacher Valerie Diggs initiated a redesign of the library space to create a gathering spot for students and teachers alike. The Chelmsford Learning Commons debuted in December 2008. It houses activities as diverse as students sharing their talents with others during "Listening Lunches" and gatherings of all school constituencies—teachers, students, and administrators—for breakfast and conversation on Wednesday mornings. The emphasis is on community and communication

(Diggs 2009). Loertscher et al. (2008), who recommend housing a variety of school services within the library, suggest that the learning commons concept is the miracle school libraries need to remain relevant to the "Google generation."

In public libraries that serve the needs of K–12 students, libraries can create a smaller-scale, similar library learning commons to address a range of students' learning and academic needs. The redesigned youth services space would be a comfortable and welcoming area where students can congregate, socialize, and work collaboratively without fear of disturbing others. Like the college students described above, K–12 students can go to the information desk and ask a librarian, staff member, or volunteer to refer them to the appropriate service or equipment. Depending on the assistance a student needs, this might include referring him to a homework tutor if a formal homework program has been established in your library, a group of computers dedicated to students in an area where a "techie" knowledgeable in library technology can help patrons, or the reference desk where a librarian can perform traditional reference services. If your library is fortunate enough to be able to afford a large number of computers, some computers should be clustered in a learning commons area or individual computers positioned amid a cluster of comfortable furniture to facilitate completing collaborative assignments. Any number of the technology-driven services discussed later in this chapter can be consolidated in the learning commons, too, including but not limited to classes in using the library's databases or creating an effective PowerPoint presentation or a writing center where students can be taught to use word processing software features to edit their writing. Some students do not need to use digital tools to complete their assignments, but one of the major advantages of a learning commons environment is the opportunity to locate equipment centrally, where it is available and easily supervised.

The Technology Center / Information Commons

The primary difference between a "learning commons" and a "technology center" or "information commons" is the accent on technological equipment as opposed to a range of services that involve, among other things, using technology. Most academic libraries have a technology center, which might include an IT help desk as well as computers and other equipment for students' use. College and university libraries organized according to the learning commons model may include a technology center in the learning commons or may refer students to a technology center located elsewhere in the building.

Many public libraries have technology centers as well, though what they contain varies widely. In many buildings, the term applies to the area in the library where public workstations are located—usually workstations with a full complement of software and any associated hardware accessories (e.g., printers, scanners). For example, the Toronto Public Library describes its Information Commons primarily in terms of the number of computers housed in the commons, the software provided, and the types of monitors available. The Princeton (New Jersey) Public Library has a technology center that includes classes, computers specifically in the center, and a "gadget garage" for equipment such as iPods, Kindles, and digital and video cameras. The Lakewood (Ohio) Public Library Technology Center provides computers, printers, databases, software, and expanded services related to technology including classes, interactive testing, and proctoring services for online classes. Other libraries, such as the relatively new Fontana Lewis Library and Technology Center in San Bernadino, California, may house a large number of computers and associated hardware and software, but they really reflect the library-as-place umbrella over diverse services, one of which is access to technology.

As magnificent as technology centers may be, they are often set up for the benefit of adult patrons, not to assist K–12 students with homework assignments, either informally or otherwise. This does not mean that students' technology needs are entirely ignored. Some libraries have set up youth services technology centers or youth computer labs that essentially serve the same purpose as the adult technology centers but with fewer computers and associated hardware and software. Some libraries identify their online pathfinders (research guides) as part of their technology centers, too. Other technology centers permit high school students to use computers in the adult centers but direct elementary and middle school students to filtered computers in the youth services areas of the library.

A fully stocked technology center that accommodates youth in proportion to their numbers in the library has enormous potential to meet students' technology needs for homework in one location—with access to the Internet for research, word processing equipment to write and print written assignments and reports, and applications to create presentations.

TECHNOLOGY IN THE LIBRARY: EQUIPMENT

In the 1957 film *Desk Set*, efficiency expert Spencer Tracy installs an "electronic brain"—an early version of a computer—in Katherine Hepburn's research department at a television network. If, as you read this, you imagine a slightly oversized desktop, think again: the "electronic brain" fills a huge room, and, in the end, not only does Hepburn and Tracy's romance blossom, but to the delight of the audience the huge machine really cannot compete with the ingenuity of human beings. Today, computers are ubiquitous in virtually every business, educational institution, and library, and few question their value to enhance, not hinder, human potential. In a movie filmed in 2011, the "electronic brain" would likely be a tool, not a replacement, for researchers.

The question for librarians today is not *whether* to provide computers for library users but *how many* and *which kind* to provide. For those of us who help young library clients with homework, the question is similar, with some nuanced differences: which types of computers, computer accessories, and software are most useful to students who do their homework in the library, and how can we secure enough computers for students' afterschool use to provide meaningful assistance to them? In the best of all possible worlds, you can get plenty of computers reserved for students to do their work and load them with a full complement of useful software. In reality, both space and cost constraints limit the numbers of computers libraries are able to purchase, and then, in turn, youth services must compete with adult services for use of this equipment to meet the needs of their constituencies. Though computer-related technology is not the only type of technology relevant to a homework help program, it is without a doubt the most important in this day and age.

Descriptions of the various types of useful technological equipment for a homework help program follow. Making a full wish list from the following items of what best meets the needs of your patrons is one of the first steps to take. However, you should also prioritize based on funding, potential funding, and space constraints in your facility. If budgetary constraints are extensive in your library, you might also evaluate the items in terms of maximizing the chances you can successfully advocate funding them by identifying which resources can be shared with adult services in the many hours they will not be used to provide homework help.

Hardware, Accessories, and Features

Computers: Desktops vs. Laptops

The first decision you face regarding computers to use in your homework help program is whether to provide stationary desktop computers, mobile laptops, or both. As to be expected, some larger systems, such as the New York Public Library and the Miami-Dade (Florida) Public Library, lend out laptops, but so do smaller systems. For example, the Milanof-Schock Library in Lancaster was the first library in Pennsylvania to lend out laptops to its patrons. For many students, desktops are more than sufficient for completing their work as long as the operating systems are compatible with those used in local school districts.

Lending laptops for use outside the building makes it difficult to preserve expensive items, since their storage and handling cannot be supervised. At the same time, the very thing that makes the use of laptops difficult to supervise—their portability—also renders them effective for school projects, especially when students need to work collaboratively. Permitting use of laptops within the library building introduces fewer problems regarding supervision of library equipment but still allows students some flexibility of where they can work.

Computers: Macs vs. PCs

The battle rages on between Apple's Mac computers and the more common Windows-based computers. Each has its devotees, though many programs are transferable between the systems. Discussions are framed in terms of cost, security, programs, and how easy the machines are to use. Whatever one chooses for personal use, the choices you make for technology in the library for homework assistance hinge on different considerations. For example, it is important to find out what your local school system uses now and what it intends to use in the future. From a student's perspective, nothing is more frustrating than spending hours creating a computer-based presentation on Elizabethan clothing for the Shakespeare unit in English class, only to find that the software used does not work on the teacher's computer. Perhaps even worse is researching and writing a report and only later discovering that it cannot be sent to school to print or to a teacher because the library's system is not compatible with the high school's system. If your local schools use Windows systems now and intend to continue to do so, it behooves you to use them in your homework help areas; similarly, if your schools use Macs, it is best if you have Macs in your homework help areas. On the other hand, Mac provides basic programs that are generally thought to be more effective for video and art projects. If one or another company offers your library free computers or software, by all means use them in your youth services areas as you do elsewhere in the library; but for homework help in particular, it is important to have equipment that is at the very least compatible with school equipment, and ideally it should be identical to what the students use at school for the same kind of work.

USB Ports and Flash Drives

All the computers used for homework should have USB ports. Students need to bring their own flash drives to the library, but they can insert them into the USB ports to download information, photographs, spreadsheets, and documents, which allows them to transfer data from one computer to another. It is helpful to provide detailed instructions online for how to use a flash drive with the library's computers.

Flash drives are also useful for staff. Free software programs can be downloaded onto flash drives, which librarians and other staff can carry with them as they circulate through the areas where students are completing their homework. The software programs can be downloaded onto computers on an as-needed basis, instead of having to load every computer with every program before opening them up for public use. As technology librarian Kelly Czarnecki writes on the YALSA blog, time and money can be saved by "using flash drives to install programs for our classes and workshops for teens. Instead of having to wait until IT installs a program on our networked computers, we have a portable program that can move around the space" (Czarnecki 2009). In addition, as librarians or staff responsible for the homework programs amass collections of various assignments from local schools, sample instructional material can be created and downloaded onto flash drives and used in the future to help students struggling with the same types of assignments.

CD/DVD Drives

CD/DVD drives are necessary in all computers used for homework. First, if your library acquires copyrighted new software that can be useful for students, CDs and DVDs are often the medium through which the software is downloaded onto your computers. In this case, it is important to have the drive to insert the software discs. It is also important to keep the CDs and DVDs safely stored for future reference in the event of damage to the computer that impedes its ability to access the program. Second, and extremely important, students need to be able to read and conduct research with the educational CD-ROMs maintained in your collection, preferably CD-ROMs that are tied to the local curricula.

Scanners

If possible, make scanners available for students who come to the library to do their homework. Scanning allows students to place into e-mail pages from texts and periodicals that they might otherwise have to copy, and it allows them to store photographs and diagrams that can help them study as well as provide visual interest in reports. Scanners can be especially helpful when students need just a few pages from a large textbook or other reference source they cannot remove from the library. In many communities across the country, learning to use a scanner properly is part of the technology curriculum. Teachers do not necessarily expect students to use scanners for homework, but having scanners in the library for students' use gives students the chance to practice a skill they are expected to master in school.

Copiers

Copiers are useful tools for the current generation of "digital natives" for the same reason they have always been useful: like scanners, they facilitate preserving for future use pages from texts and periodicals that are otherwise expensive or cannot be removed from the library. This information can be used to study or can be (physically as opposed to digitally) cut and pasted into a report. Furthermore, having a copier may reduce the number of books that are stolen or mutilated (Vaillancourt 2000, 35).

Printers

Printers are important to homework help for two main reasons. If your users do not have Internet access at home, printers allow them to take home pages they need for further study or to complete assignments. In addition, increasingly teachers are strongly suggesting if not requiring students to type their written assignments. By providing computers with word processing software, libraries facilitate this process. However, if students cannot print their work or don't have flash drives of their own, or if the library software is incompatible with the school software, the computers are of little use to the students. To a teacher's ear, "I left my assignment on the library computer" sounds like another excuse—a novel one, perhaps, but in the end just an excuse.

Assuming your library does choose to offer printing services for computer users, including students doing their homework, you also need to consider whether to have only black-and-white printers or color printers as well, a choice frequently determined by cost constraints. Color printing allows students to understand differentiations defined by color, such as those in graphs or maps, to reproduce artwork accurately, to illustrate concepts exemplified by color differentiation (e.g., rainbows, sunsets, or various aspects of anatomy), and to produce assignments that include color for the same reasons listed above and for visual interest. But color printers and color printing are more expensive than monochrome, both for the initial purchase and the cost of operation.

What to charge for printing is another decision you need to make for your homework help program. In many instances, the cost to young users is the same as what adults incur when they use printers, but some systems, such as the Ozark–Dale County (Alabama) Public Library, allow all K–12 students to print at no charge for school assignments. To the extent that you can convince your library administrators and oversight board to adopt similar policies, you do a great service for your young patrons. Allowing them to print for free encourages them to use fully the computer technology you make available and permits them to extend the benefits of that technology when they go home to study or hand in assignments at school.

Combination Machines

Depending on the funding and space available in your library, you might consider using a machine that incorporates a scanner, a copier, and a printer all in one rather than purchasing and finding space for separate equipment.

Digital Visual Equipment

"Film and tape as recording media are dead. No one uses nondigital cameras or audio recorders any more." So reports Jennifer Nelson (2009), technology applications coordinator for the Hennepin (Minnesota) Public Library administration, in an ALA Connect posting. Instead, libraries that wish to provide technology to permit students to explore audiovisual project creation for homework assignments need to examine the media used in schools as well as in related professions. Consider including digital cameras, video equipment, and webcams.

Software

You have fought the battle to have a large proportion of your computers dedicated for student use after school each day for homework help purposes. Now you have to decide what to put on those computers. The software you load into your machines should be selected, just as the hardware, on the basis of what students are going to do with it—or what you are going to let them do with it. For the purposes of doing their homework, students use computers for two major reasons: to seek and retrieve information; and to create documents, presentations, and other written assignments. Students certainly use computers for other purposes as well, which I discuss later.

Web Browsers

Most people, no matter how old they are, think Internet when they think about finding and retrieving information on a computer. Students are no exception.

In a study of student use of the Internet, the Pew Charitable Trust found that, by 2004, 87 percent of middle and high school students had Internet access either at home or elsewhere (including libraries), and the vast majority of them used the Internet for homework (Lenhart et al. 2005).

One important step is to make sure you have a useful web browser on the Internet access computers available for student use, which for Windows-based computers usually means, at the very least, Internet Explorer software. First introduced in 1995 with Microsoft's Windows 95 package, Explorer is the most widely used web browser today. Mozilla's Firefox is Explorer's biggest competitor, and many libraries download it. One of the major advantages of Firefox is that it is open-source software, which means that programmers can adapt it for particular uses, independent of any vendor's (such as Microsoft's) control.[1] Internet articles and blogs abound with comparisons between the respective advantages of Explorer and Firefox, with discussions focusing on specific features, such as the inclusion or exclusion of a "go" button, and on security. Google also recently introduced free browser software that has been gaining in popularity: Goggle Chrome. If you have Macs, you will likely use Safari, the licensed Apple web browser. Some libraries limit their browser software to the dominant Explorer, and I recommend using it for homework help programs if it is the browser used by your local schools. If you choose to use a different browser than the one used in schools, at the very least post instructions that outline the few differences between the programs (e.g., how to exit the program) so the students who are not familiar with both can easily adapt to your browser. The most important feature of all is that whatever you select should be compatible with the software used in your local schools.

Databases and CD-ROMs

A collection of educational CD-ROMs and subscriptions to educational databases are among the most valuable assets for students in the library. Many teens have computers at home or in school computer labs where they can access the Internet. What the Internet does *not* offer but the library does is preselected, accurate, detailed educational information. In fact, as of 2008, 87 percent of all libraries subscribed to databases, providing content in virtually every school subject, and many state library boards used LSTA and state funds to invest in these databases (ALA 2009b). Many libraries make these databases available via their websites, too (see chapter 5).

Several sources are available to help you select databases for your library. Rose Nelson, systems librarian of the Colorado Alliance of Research Libraries, has produced an especially helpful and current list of sources that review online databases and e-products (see appendix A). Coordinate your selection with your local schools' curricula and house copies of these and reference CD-ROMs in the homework help areas in your library.

Word Processing

From the perspective of providing homework help, the most important feature of the word processing software you use on library computers is its compatibility with school computers. The most commonly used software is a recent version of Microsoft Word. Not all Word programs are compatible with others, however, and it is extremely important to contact your local schools to confirm that assignments created on library computers can be revised and printed on school computers. If different schools in your district use different programs, try to have all of the programs available for students so they can use the same programs in the library that they use in school.

The second important feature of your word processing program software is that it be able to facilitate the rich applications students need to write papers and create graphs, charts, and presentations. Some libraries provide publishing programs, too.

Even though libraries may vary the services or programs they offer on one set of computers or another, such as the level of Internet access, most libraries choose to load all computers in the building with the same word processing programs. For example, at this writing all computers at the St. Charles (Illinois) Public Library have Microsoft Office 2007 software, though Internet access varies, and at the West Palm Beach (Florida) Public Library all computers have Microsoft Office, including the computers in the library's Kid Space. Some libraries, such as the Lakewood (Illinois) Public Library, have several word processing programs on their computers. Lakewood provides both the licensed Microsoft Office 2007 program and Open Office 2 Suite, an open-source program that offers word processing, spreadsheets, graphics management, and presentations.

A final consideration when you select your word processing program is the type of spell checker you select. Research shows that students who struggle with English are more likely to succeed in reading and math than in spelling, which impacts their ability to write effectively (Glasgow et al. 2006). Spell checkers can help instruct by modeling proper spelling, but those who are just learning or struggle with the language, such as English-language learners and those with learning disabilities, need a spell checker program that can accommodate a wider range of spelling guesses for the program to serve this purpose. If the groups of students coming to your library for homework help includes a large percentage of immigrants, you should investigate downloading spell checkers designed for English-language learners who may otherwise not receive the same benefit from your software as native English speakers.

Managing Images

What do pictures have to do with homework? Even if we put aside the kindergartner's assignment to find photos of objects that begin with, say, the letter *T*, students do use images when they do homework. Some assignments are directly focused on images, such as those for various technology, computer, or art classes, but images are also useful for providing visual interest in reports. These constitute visual text in presentations and can illustrate students' knowledge of various facts, such a diagram of a major organ system or geological formation. Software choices to provide editing, formatting, and authoring images include the better-known licensed programs such as Adobe Photoshop Elements and Microsoft's Digital Image Suite and free and open-source programs such as GNU Image Manipulation Program (GIMP).

Open-Source and Free Software

Several open-source and free software programs are mentioned above, but it is worth noting that some information services professionals advocate increasing the use of software that does not require payment for using the licensed source code. One resource is John Houser's April 2009 issue of ALA's *Library Technology Reports,* "Open Source Public Workstations in Libraries." Houser, an open-source expert, describes how these systems and software can provide equally useful applications at a lower cost to libraries. Others have a different perspective. Library consultant Eric Morgan (2009) reviews various open-source software and writes that open-source library software is "only 'as free as a free kitten.' . . . Free kittens do not come without costs," such as the time and money it costs to care for them. The library does not have to pay to buy the software or systems, but development, maintenance, training, and sometimes the hardware you need to use with the open-source software and systems bring affiliated expenses. To repeat the mantra that runs throughout this book, if your priority is providing useful homework help to your young patrons, the choices you make for the homework help program should largely be driven by what is in use at your local schools so that you are supporting the formal learning experience with less formal assistance in the library and so that the student's assignments are easily transferable to school computers.

Adaptive or Assistive Technology

No one type of disabled patron requiring one set of adaptive technologies exists. "Special needs" vary widely, from those caused by cognitive disabilities such as Down syndrome, phenylketonuria, or the results of brain trauma to physical challenges such as visual impairment or cerebral palsy. Given the range of challenges, what helps one student requiring adaptive technology may not necessarily be useful to another. In the planning stages, consult with your constituents to find out the range of needs in your community, because using the Internet and computers to do their homework is just as important to your disabled patrons as it is to patrons who do not face physical or cognitive challenges. Consult with the local schools, too, to coordinate your adaptive technology choices with them. This may reduce the time your staff spends training students to use the technology in the library, and consistency between what students use at school and what they use at the library makes the process of doing homework easier for your patrons.

Students with physical disabilities need accessible workstations and software. Those who are wheelchair bound or have motor challenges benefit from easily adjustable chair and table heights and computer monitor position. If students have difficulty with fine motor coordination, trackballs, joysticks, oversized touch pads, larger keys, and switches are good alternatives to the traditional mouse or keypad. Because the process of typing into the computer can be especially arduous for students with certain kinds of physical disabilities, computer word prediction programs are useful, similar to those employed by mobile phone texting programs. These require fewer keystrokes to type text. Students who cannot use their hands can tap keys or computer screens with a pointer that attaches to the head or other hands-free device. Visually impaired students can benefit from magnification, which may be available through the operating software on your computer; voice-activated programs; and braille keypads. Screen readers, which interpret text on the computer screen into speech or braille, are also helpful for visually impaired students, as are programs that allow students to scan printed material into the computer for conversion into speech or braille. Hearing-impaired students appreciate closed-caption software, which may also be available through the computer operating system.

Students with cognitive disabilities may also experience physical difficulties with technology, and some of the same assistive technologies, such as alternatives to the mouse or small keypad, word prediction software, and voice-activated programs, are useful to them, too. Some adaptive technology is designed specifically for students with cognitive disabilities, such as programs designed to increase reading speed by highlighting text as the student hears it. Other programs can measure reading fluency.

ALA provides information on assistive technology in libraries that can help you plan technology for the homework help program: the Association and Specialized and Cooperative Library Agencies' Tip Sheet 11 is a general overview of the topic, and the Office for Literacy and Outreach Services posts useful links, papers, and resources online. The National Institute on Disability and Rehabilitative Research of the U.S. Department of Education assigned AbleData to maintain a huge online list of assistive technology products that can help with ideas about what might work in your library.[2] The products are grouped by disability type as well as specific spheres of assistance, such as computers or education.

On your library website, let your patrons know which assistive technologies you offer for students to use for homework and where you offer them. A perusal of several state library association or county public library systems showed that adaptive technology is offered at local branches, but many of those local library websites made no mention of their adaptive equipment.

TECHNOLOGY IN THE LIBRARY: SERVICES

No doubt some of your young patrons come to the library fully informed about how to use some or all of the technologies you offer in your building. Many, however, do not know how to use them *capably* so that they benefit fully from the access you provide. Therefore, in addition to providing the technologies themselves, it is important to provide services associated with those technologies. This support generally falls into two categories: information literacy support and Internet access.

Information Literacy

"Information literacy" is a current buzzword in both education and information services circles. For the librarian, "[information] literacy gets at the core of what we do, which is connecting people and information" (Jones and Shoemaker, 2001, 115). Students need IT advice to learn how to use the equipment you offer, and after they can use the equipment they need to learn what to do with the deluge of information they encounter. AASL addressed the challenges of instructing students in information literacy as early as the 1990s and in the more recently released Standards for the 21st-Century Learner, in which specific information literacy skills are outlined (AASL 2007). The major steps involved are to "define the need for information, initiate the search strategy, locate the resources, assess and comprehend the information, interpret the information, communicate the information, and evaluate the product and process" (Brooks-Young 2006, 16). AASL also provides a list of resources for literacy instruction on its website; so does the National Forum on Information Literacy.[3]

Until the late 1990s into the turn of the century, the job of teaching information literacy fell primarily to schools, K–12 libraries, and institutes of higher education, where limited help was provided with computers and other forms of information literacy. But youth librarians began to recognize that students needed more than access to the Internet; they needed help navigating it. Information literacy instruction expanded, especially instruction on how to conduct searches effectively and evaluate data.

All of the models for teaching information literacy are premised on tapping and strengthening the same metacognitive processes emphasized in education today (see chapter 6). They involve planning the search process, conducting the search for information, evaluating and interpreting information, and using the retrieved information effectively. Before you begin to plan how you would like to structure your information literacy instruction model, contact the local schools' librarians and computer teachers and examine the technology curricula. If the school uses specific models when students learn information literacy in the classroom or the school library, you should use the same structure when you provide information literacy instruction for students in the public library. You may want to tweak and improve upon the methods used by the schools, but you provide the most effective homework help support for your users if the processes you discuss and language you use in the library are consistent with what they learn in school. Once you decide the approach to take with students to demonstrate information literacy, delineate each step clearly and have examples on hand to illustrate each one for your patrons.

Below are several types of information literacy instruction programs in place in libraries across the country. Examine your library's budget, space, and staffing to consider which will work best in your institution.

One-on-One Assistance

Two kinds of one-on-one assistance can be implemented. The first is informal and happens every day in the library. Librarians are approached for advice on how to use computers or databases, or they approach students who seem to be having difficulty. They may suggest search terminology after an initial reference interview. The second kind of one-on-one assistance is more formal. Students call, chat, e-mail, or sign up for a session with a librarian to obtain instruction on information literacy skills. In some cases this instruction can be specific to certain kinds of projects. For example, the Public Library of Charlotte and Mecklenberg County (North Carolina) allows students to schedule an appointment with a reference librarian to receive assistance with the research process. The librarian helps the student figure out how to begin, which resources are available, and how to complete the assignment effectively. The Winchester (Massachusetts) Public Library offers a similar program called "Book a Librarian."

For technical assistance, one low-cost option is to recruit, train, and oversee a team of "techie" volunteers or assistants. Teens are a good source for these assistants. In fact, teens often look to the library for volunteer opportunities to meet schools' or other organizations' community service requirement. Using library techies who help other students navigate computers is an excellent way to engage your knowledgeable teens at the same time you provide a valuable service to all your young patrons. Walter and Meyers (2003) highlight a program in King County, Washington, that involves paying teens for this purpose.

Classes Coordinated with Schools

Most cooperative programs that involve school visits to the public library, according to an ALA review of school/public library cooperative programs, involve librarians reading to classes or a general visit to the library.[4] If information literacy is mentioned in the various reports from librarians, it is only indirectly. Some libraries, however, have specifically introduced an information literacy component to this traditional service. For example, the Multnomah County (Oregon) Library School Corps offers a range of presentations for various grade levels on online research tools, including how to use the computerized catalog, how to use the library website, using library databases, Internet safety, and how to use the chat homework help program. These presentations last anywhere from ten to forty-five minutes, depending on the topic. Another example is a service that was offered by the Las Vegas–Clark County (Nevada) Library District, "Web on Wheels," a program to conduct free assemblies to introduce students to library resources, including databases and research tools. Libraries that already have information literacy interactive presentations prepared can easily transfer their mini-lessons to the library building itself and demonstrate for students how to use the equipment in the library to enhance their homework.

Classes at the Library

Many libraries offer information literacy classes, though not all do so specifically with the idea of helping students in mind. Three examples are the

Nacogdoches (Texas) Public Library, which offers free computer classes to all patrons age twelve and up; the Old Bridge (New Jersey) Public Library, which offers forty-five-minute classes on computer use for children; and the Nashville (Tennessee) Public Library. Nacogdoches's classes range from the most basic introduction to computer use and e-mail to instruction in the use of more complex software programs, such as presentation software and spreadsheets. Nashville offers a class just prior to the start of the school year to introduce students to library resources, including online resources and databases. If your library does not offer classes specifically designed to improve kids' information literacy in such a way that homework improves, you might consider addressing some of the following topics in afterschool or early evening programs and recruit K–12 students to participate:

Keyboarding. Students who have computers at home master keyboarding at a fairly early age. Other students depend on time in the school computer lab or media center or trips to the library after school to learn and practice this critical computer skill. Offering keyboarding in the library is one way to close this aspect of the information literacy gap.

Using library databases. A general class can be held, or you can divide classes up by age group or topic. The library's subscription databases are useful for completing homework only if students know how to use them.

Using the Internet for homework. Almost every article about young people and technology emphasizes how adept they are with iPods and cell phones, IM-ing, and using computers alone or in a multitasking frenzy. However, as Walter (2001, 79) points out, "many researchers have found that although most children do indeed approach computers more confidently than adults do, they do not necessarily use them effectively for information retrieval." Students benefit from learning how to articulate Internet searches, how to evaluate the trustworthiness of websites, where to look on the Internet for collections of useful academic information, and how to evaluate the information once they find it. For example, many students do not realize that the ".com" or ".net" suffixes in a web address usually indicate a commercial concern, whereas ".edu" usually indicates an academic institution, "k12.[state abbreviation].us" usually means a public school system, ".org" means a nonprofit organization, and ".gov" is a sign that you have reached a government website. Similarly, kids may not realize that the ".uk," ".il," or ".it" at the end of a web address means that it originates, respectively, in England, Israel, and Italy, and that other abbreviations indicate other countries. Knowing this can help students figure out if the information on a given website is trustworthy or useful.

A series of classes in which the instructor models how to use the Internet to respond to specific types of homework assignments can be especially useful to students. For example, classes might include using the Internet to conduct research for a report on a specific topic (e.g., a country or scientific principle), to enhance an essay assignment, to retrieve noncopyrighted images for a poster or visual presentation, or to take practice tests to hone skills of various kinds, even at the elementary school level.

Internet safety. Although kids are proficient at using the Internet, often they are unaware of or naïve about the dangers of providing personal information online, such as their names, addresses, schools, or photographs. Parents and students alike benefit from an understanding of how to use the Internet safely. Many law enforcement agencies and private organizations concerned with predators on the Internet provide online hints for how to address safety and security.

How to cite information from the Internet. One of the marvelous things about articles by librarians on the Internet is that they are almost always accompanied by instructions on how to cite the article. This is not the case for most other websites. However, students are frequently required to cite information properly.

Using specific software. Students who are facile with word processing programs and social networks are not necessarily capable users of various image-editing or spreadsheet programs. The reverse is also true. The library can offer a series of mini-classes specifically designed to show young patrons how software can be used to enhance the homework process and final production of long-term assignments.

How parents can help their children use technology for homework. Courses for parents do not directly help your young patrons improve homework, but, just as parents can be a source of information in your needs assessment, you can work with them to improve their children's informational literacy. Information online abounds for parents. ALA and the U.S. Department of Education offer valuable websites with resources for parents to help their children with the Internet, and similar advice can be found on some library and school websites as well.[5] It would be very useful to provide classes for parents whose children are "digital natives" to help them become comfortable with their own and their children's use of the Internet for homework.

Programs in Other Languages

One question to keep in mind as you create a list of classes and services to offer is whether bilingual services are appropriate. Communities with large concentrations of immigrant groups for whom English is not the native language would benefit from information literacy instruction in their first languages.

For this reason, many libraries in California and Florida communities with significant Latino populations offer most if not all of their programs in both English and Spanish. One example of responding to language needs of the local population was implemented at the Long Beach (California) Public Library, which opened a family center staffed by bilingual, college-age, paid "homework and literacy helpers" to meet the needs—including information literacy instruction—of Latino and Cambodian families from low-performing schools.

Internet Access

The Internet is an invaluable research tool for students. It is a source of information and of visual, aural, and written text. It brings millions of tidbits of data to our fingertips—now, here. It allows us to create material and share it with our friends and with the world. The Internet is also socializing where no adult can oversee content. It is "hanging out" on the virtual corner, sometimes at all hours of the night. It is sensory overload. Hoaxes. False information and rumors. At its worst, the Internet is pornography, predators, and computer viruses. Therein lies one of the main controversies to face youth librarians: if we provide access to the Internet for young people, especially on computers we choose to delineate as solely for the use of students after school, should we limit what material they can access and how they are allowed to use the computers?

Crossing the Digital Divide: Why Libraries Should
Provide Internet Access for Students

The first question to ask is whether libraries should provide Internet access for students at all. As Sullivan (2005, 106) points out, it is not really a library "service" in the traditional sense of the word: "It is not really part of the collection, as there is no selection process and the library does not own, or even own the rights to, the information it contains." Still, if libraries are to meet the information needs of students working on their homework, Internet access is fundamental. As noted earlier, teachers in the majority of school districts in the country give assignments that involve using the Internet. Even though 60 percent of U.S. households had Internet access as of 2008, the percentage dropped to half when households with lower incomes were examined, and the numbers were even lower for Latino and African American households (ALA 2009b). This is the digital divide, a chasm between the abundant access to digital information among white, wealthier families and the relative dearth of this access among minority, immigrant, and poorer families. Libraries, which are often the sole source of free Internet access in their communities, help their patrons cross that divide, a critical service to students who would otherwise be unable to compete with their classmates. It also offers those students the opportunity to participate in the increasing number of online courses offered by school districts across the country.

An example of a system that responded to the needs of students for Internet access is the Michael and Susan Dell Wired for Youth Centers established in 2000 in ten branches of the Austin (Texas) Public Library in low-income communities. The centers were created specifically to ensure students in these communities access to computers to conduct research and do their homework. A key aspect of this program is that is it unstructured, allowing students to determine themselves how they use the Internet, with support from library staff.

If we consider that library usage is still consistently highest during after-school hours, with use of computers and the Internet also highest during those hours, then the need for this kind of service among young patrons is evident. Furthermore, one study found that teens, in particular, prefer to log on from home, but when they need to use a computer they are increasingly likely to go to the library to do so (Lenhart et al. 2005).

Should the Material Students Access on the Internet Be Limited?

With the enactment of the Communications Decency Act of 1996, the Child Online Protection Act of 1993, and the Children's Internet Protection Act (CIPA) of 1993, the federal government answered this question. Receipt of much-needed federal e-funds is contingent on some kind of filtering for pornography. ALA has created a website to help you explore both the history of CIPA and resources to help you plan to implement filters in your library to accommodate government requirements (see "CIPA and Internet Policy Resources," below). The site includes links to worksheets for planning purposes, advice from other librarians, and descriptions of best practices. Among the suggestions presented are blocking photos rather than full pages and linking log-on information to age records for the patron so that adults are offered both filtered or unfiltered material while minors have access only to filtered material.

Not all libraries filter. WebJunction includes a page on CIPA filtering that documents different libraries' experiences and policies. Linda Mielke of Carroll County (Maryland) Public Library reports her library filters in order to receive federal funds, which the system uses to improve Internet services (Mielke 2004), and the San Francisco (California) Public Library forgoes federal funding and abides by the local law banning filtering on computers used by adults and teens (Anderson 2005). WebJunction also maintains an article by CIPA expert Robert Bocher and librarian-attorney Mary Minow on the significance of the 2003 Supreme Court ruling regarding CIPA (Bocher and Minow 2004).

How relevant is filtering to providing access to the Internet for homework? Not very. Virtually no homework assignments involve students sifting through pornographic material. But if you provide students with Internet access, then your library must consider the CIPA limitations when it designates computers for student use. Many libraries address this by separating computers by children's and adult area.

Should Libraries Limit What Students Can Do on the Internet?

Students use the Internet for homework all the time, especially for research. Ahhhh. The Internet is a good thing for students doing their homework. But in a list of what young people do on the Internet, activities include IM-ing, gaming, dating, looking for housing or jobs, creating content, peer-to-peer networking, searching for cultural information, rating things, and accessing adult content (Rainie 2006). This is not so good, many think. How can youth librarians intent on securing Internet access for students keep them focused on the tasks at hand—their homework—without letting them get distracted by these other temptations that amount to socializing via computer? The answer: they shouldn't. One of the biggest mistakes librarians can make, according to research conducted by the MacArthur Foundation's Digital Youth Project, is to prevent students from using the Internet for social and recreational purposes (Ito et al. 2008).

One reason to support student use of socializing online from the library, even if they start out using computers for homework, is that some students use these mechanisms to enhance academic and intellectual pursuits. Some students explore fields of interest to "go beyond what they have access to at

CIPA AND INTERNET POLICY RESOURCES

- ALA CIPA-Related Resources, www.ala.org/ala/issues advocacy/advocacy/federallegislation/cipa/alaciparelated resources.cfm
- WebJunction, CIPA and Filtering, www.webjunction.org/ cipa/-/resources/wjarticles
- ALA, Internet Use Policies, www.ala.org/ala/aboutala/offices/ oif/ifissues/issuesrelatedlinks/internetusepolicies.cfm

school or in their local community. Online groups enable youth to connect to peers who share specialized and niche interests of various kinds," including creative and academic pursuits. When students connect like this, their tinkering improves their information literacy skills. Other students use IM-ing and social networking programs to communicate with each other when they are collaborating on school projects or to contact teachers. Most important of all, however, "adults should facilitate young people's engagement with digital media. Contrary to adult perceptions, while hanging out online, youth are picking up basic social and technical skills they need to fully participate in contemporary society. Erecting barriers to participation deprives teens of access to these forms of learning" (Ito et al. 2008).

The authors of the MacArthur Foundation report recommend that educational institutions explore using relatively new digital networking media for more formal educational purposes, but at this point the major emphasis is encouraging participation. Students cannot compete with their classmates in the modern world if they cannot communicate with them and participate in the online community.

Internet Use Policy

Every library needs a fully fleshed-out, practical Internet use policy for all users, including students. Policies should address which computers are available to which age groups and during what hours; what kinds of materials, if any, are restricted from one or more computers; time limits if necessary; how to reserve computer time; what equipment the library offers (e.g., flash drives must be brought by the user, not provided by the library); restrictions on downloading programs onto the library computers; and disclaimers to prevent library liability in the event a user does not follow the library policy. To view sample policies, librarians can go to virtually any public library website, or look at sample policies posted on the ALA website. Table 2 includes examples of specific issues addressed in some of the policies highlighted on this website.

It is important to post the policy for students or distribute it to them, but do so gently; if students are handed a brusque list of don'ts the instant they come into the library, they may be discouraged from coming back.

✳   ✳   ✳

Some argue that students hardly need to come to the library any more to access information, but the fact that millions of youths have logged onto computers from libraries refutes that position. When they do come to the library to do their homework, the technology you offer and the way you organize

TABLE 2

Sample Library Internet Policies

POLICY TOPIC	LANGUAGE USED IN LIBRARY INTERNET POLICIES
Internet accuracy	The Library has no control over the information accessed through the Internet and cannot be held responsible for its content.[a]
	Library staff cannot control the availability of information links that often change quickly and unpredictably. Not all sources on the Internet provide accurate, complete or current information.[b]
Chat and e-mail access	Access to chat is allowed at a limited number of computer stations at each branch. Chat is not allowed on computers in the children's or young adult departments. Parental permission shall be obtained for minors wishing to use chat on the Library's designated chat computers. Access to e-mail is allowed on all computers except the Funding Information Center computers at the Library Center.[a]
	The Library permits access to personal email and chat rooms by adults and minors.[c]
Downloading files	Customers may not download any files onto the hard drives of library computers. Downloads should be made directly onto a floppy disk, available for purchase for $1.00 each.[d]
	The Library prohibits: attempts to download or make copies of unauthorized files, attempts to hack or crack Library or remote servers, displays of web site images which are pornographic or defined by Maryland State Law as obscene.[c]
	Users may not attempt to reconfigure systems or software, or in any way interfere with or disrupt the current system or network set-up and services.[e]

| **Filtering** | The Burlington County Library System provides Internet access on PCs which are filtered appropriately for youth and adult areas of the library. Each PC is labeled to indicate its level of filtering. Even with filtering, some Internet sites that are inappropriate in a library setting may be displayed. Because the library is a public place, library staff has the authority to end an Internet session when such material displays.[d] |

(Filtering) software . . . may also block access to material that is constitutionally protected, for example, information about breast cancer or AIDS. Federal law allows the Library to unblock individual websites that customers believe should not have been filtered. . . . (The) Library will disable the entire filter for adult patrons age 17 and over upon request.[c]

In compliance with the Children's Internet Protection Act (CIPA), Jefferson-Madison Regional Library provides Internet workstations equipped with filtering/blocking technology. However, the library recognizes that filtering/blocking technology is not a completely reliable means of protection from materials that may be offensive, controversial or illegal.[f]

Parental responsibility

Users age twelve and younger shall have access to Internet stations in Children's Services when accompanied by a parent/guardian or an individual over the age of eighteen appointed by the parent/guardian (parental appointment must be verified in writing).[b]

It is both the right and the responsibility of parents and legal guardians to guide their own children's usage of library resources in accordance with individual family beliefs. The library has created Web pages for children . . . and young adults . . . which provide content and links to other Web sites that parents and legal guardians may find appropriate for their children.[e]

Parents and guardians are responsible for monitoring Internet access for their children ages 17 and under.[g]

Library staff is not in a position to supervise juveniles' use of the Internet.[f]

cont.

Table 2 (cont.)

POLICY TOPIC	LANGUAGE USED IN LIBRARY INTERNET POLICIES
Time limits	Each location provides several computers with various initial time periods, from 30 minutes to 2 hours. These limits will be extended automatically in 15 minute increments up to double the initial time period, if no one is waiting.[d]
	Unless otherwise posted, computer sessions are limited to 30 minutes when others are waiting. During busy times, staff may require half-hour intervals between sessions by the same computer user.[f]
Privacy	Users may not invade the privacy of others. Each customer has the right to a quiet and organized work space.[e]
	Jefferson-Madison Regional Library cannot guarantee computer viewing privacy, nor can the library guarantee the privacy of information sent or received over the Internet.[f]
	To preserve user privacy, the Library will never share, sell, or rent individual personal information it gathers, except for the purpose of recovering overdue items and fines or as ordered by subpoena under the USA PATRIOT ACT.[c]
	Hennepin County Library supports the right to privacy and confidentiality of Library customers in accordance with the Minnesota Data Practices Act.[g]

[a]Springfield Greene County Library, Springfield, MO. Internet Access Policy. http://thelibrary.springfield.missouri.org/abpit/internet.cfm.

[b]Morrison Reeves Library, IN. Internet Use Agreement. www.mrl.lib.in.us/accept.html.

[c]Enoch Pratt Free Library, Baltimore, MD. Internet Use Policy. www.prattlibrary.org/about/index.aspx?id=2298&mark=Internet+Policy.

[d]Burlington County Library System, NJ. Internet and Computer Use Policy. www.bcls.lib.nj.us/about/policy_internet.shtml.

[e]San Jose Public Library, CA. Internet Access Policy. www.sjlibrary.org/legal/internet.htm.

[f]Jefferson Madison Regional Library, Charlottesville, VA. Internet Services. http://jmrl.org/li-internet.htm.

[g]Hennepin County Library, MN. Internet Public Use Policy. www.hclib.org/pub/info/board_policies/internet_public_use_policy.cfm.

it determine whether you are meeting students' needs in general and their homework needs in particular. The learning commons model provides an organizational structure for a welcoming environment with multiple arrangements for individual and collaborative work and a sense of community that can include homework assistance. A technology center offers a similar centralization of equipment and software that is useful for homework help. The technologies you choose, both hardware and software, should be compatible with the technologies taught to and used by students in their local schools so that homework is transferable to school computers and library homework help bolsters school learning.

Technology-related services are also quite important, including providing information literacy instruction in formal classes and through informal one-on-one assistance. Among the most important technology-related services in the library building are free access to the Internet, especially for those students who have no other access to this vital information and communication pathway, and assistance in using the Internet effectively. Students not only need this access to complete assignments, but their participation in online social networks, e-mail, Twitter, blogging, and IM-ing enables them to learn digital communication skills that are necessary if they are to compete in the digital age.

Finally, your administrators, your staff, and you should carefully define your policies regarding how your young patrons can use the wealth of technology available in the library building to ensure safe, efficient, and equitable distribution of these very valuable resources among the students who come to your building to do their homework.

Notes

1. According to Richard Boss, an expert in library technology who prepares *Tech Notes* for the Public Library Association, "the term 'open source' refers to software that is free and that includes the original source code used to create it so that users can modify it" (2008, 1). Users can adjust the program to fit individualized needs—or pay someone to do it for them—but they do not need to consult or employ the vendor to customize the programs. The Open Source Initiative provides a more detailed definition of "open source" at www.opensource.org/docs/osd.

2. Sources on assistive technology: ALA, Association and Specialized and Cooperative Library Agencies, Tip Sheet 11: "Library Accessibility and Assistive Technology: What You Need To Know," www.ala.org/ala/mgrps/divs/ascla/asclaprotools/accessibilitytipsheets/tipsheets/11%20ASSISTIVE%20TECHNOL.pdf; ALA, Office for Literacy and Outreach Services, "Services to People with Disabilities," www.ala.org/ala/aboutala/offices/olos/servicespeopledisabilities.cfm;

U.S. Department of Education, AbleData, "Products," www.abledata.com/able data.cfm?pageid=19327&ksectionid=19327.

3. Resources for literacy instruction: AASL, Essential Links: Resources for School Library Media Program Development, "Information Literacy," aasl.ala.org/essen tiallinks/index.php?title=Information_Literacy; National Forum on Information Literacy, www.infolit.org.

4. AASL/ALSC/YALSA Interdivisional Committee on School/Public Library Cooperation, "School/Public Library Cooperative Programs," www.ala.org/ala/ mgrps/divs/alsc/initiatives/partnerships/coopacts/schoolplcoopprogs.cfm.

5. Resources for parents: ALA, "Especially for Young People and Their Parents, 2007," www.ala.org/ala/aboutala/offices/oif/foryoungpeople/childrenparents/ especiallychildren.cfm; U.S. Department of Education, "Parents' Guide to the Internet," 1997, www.ed.gov/pubs/parents/internet/index.html.

FIVE

Technology from Remote Locations for Homework Help

IN THE 1960s *Star Trek* episode "All Our Yesterdays," Kirk, Spock, and McCoy find themselves on a remote planet in the company of a huge computer library that contains the entire history and knowledge of the planet Sarpeidon. The library is managed by Mr. Atoz, the only—and understandably highly stressed—librarian. The main service provided by Mr. Atoz is to help patrons use the library to access different eras in the planet's past and transport them back to these time periods to escape an impending nova about to destroy the planet. The "library" of this episode was a marvel indeed; its diverse collection was about as complete as any patron could hope for, and it could be accessed via a technology that was beginning to come into its own in the real world of the 1960s, computer science. But one aspect of the episode was quite atavistic: to access the vast collections managed by Mr. Atoz, patrons had to go to the library.

For almost all of the vast history of libraries, the only way to access information was to physically go to where the information was stored. Many, many patrons still do so—but they don't always have to. Over the course of the twentieth century, information services transformed rapidly in response to each technological advance that facilitated the storage of and access to information and each new method for people to communicate with one another. Telephone reference has existed in one form or another for almost eighty years. In the 1960s, the U.S. National Library of Medicine created its MEDLARS database for the medical community, and scientists, medical researchers, engineers, and defense contractors began using online systems. In 1971 the very first digitization of text was carried out by Michael Hart at the University of Illinois, thus beginning the oldest online digital collection, Project Gutenberg. During the 1970s and 1980s, library automation flourished. In the 1990s, the first e-mail reference services were introduced, and in 1994 the Helsinki (Finland) City Library put the very first library website on the World Wide Web. Now libraries and much of the information stored in them can be accessed via websites, chats, blogs, RSS feeds, and social networks. The library's walls are dissolving.

The Web's introduction into the world of homework changed the entire landscape of how children do their homework and how libraries provide assistance to students. As "Shifted Librarian" Jenny Levine (2006) points out, today's kids, "millennials," expect information to come to them, not the other way around, whether they are accessing information for fun, such as gaming, or for completing schoolwork. Libraries' web presence enables them to respond to these expectations. The key to providing successful homework help to remote locations instead of in the library is to have "a virtual branch library that rivals our physical locations in design, customer service, depth of collections and browsability" (Jeske 2005).

In this chapter I explore ways in which this kind of academic support and homework help can be provided to patrons in remote locations via online library services. The types of technologies libraries can use on the Web to provide homework help can be divided into two categories: technologies that involve one-way communication from the library to the user, and technologies that involve two-way communication between the library and the user or among library users.

ONE-WAY COMMUNICATION: FROM THE LIBRARY TO THE STUDENT

The most traditional way of providing online assistance to young patrons as they complete their homework is to create a website rich with links to information relevant to schoolwork. The key to providing useful and successful assistance online is to coordinate the services you provide and the links you create with the curricula in local schools and to organize it in such a way that students can access it. It does not help your patrons, for example, if your library has a magnificent subject guide for elementary school students on the country of Ghana, but your school system recently removed the quarter-long unit on Ghana altogether from the third-grade world studies curricula.

Organizing Library Web Pages for Homework Help

Although students use the Internet as a virtual textbook and reference library, only 20 percent of students in an OCLC survey found library websites worthwhile sources of Internet information (De Rosa et al. 2005). These facts, combined with rapidly changing technologies and online opportunities, have some serious implications for the effectiveness of library websites as a source of assistance to students. Yes, students are using the Internet, but no, they are not using library websites. What should we do about it?

Some, like former YALSA president Linda Braun, feel that perhaps "instead of making the teens come to the library web site it's time to start being where the teens are and perhaps give up the clunky web presence that rarely can compete with Google or Wikipedia" (Braun 2007). Similar views are expressed by advocates of Library 2.0, which has applications for homework assistance. On the other hand, students prefer to use familiar resources for information, and they want to find that information quickly (Gross 2004; Large 2004). This implies an important role for libraries websites, which can be designed specifically to respond to these preferences by becoming familiar repositories for easily accessible, accurate, current, curriculum-based information for students.

Most libraries with websites have a children's or teens' website or both. Because youth services involve a range of activities related to the library and information that have nothing to do with school assignments, it is important to distinguish homework assistance. This can be accomplished either by creating a separate homework web page (or pages) or by including links to homework help on the youth services' websites. A separate homework page better reflects student preferences. Students like to have a "landmark page" from which they make "excursions" when they search for information on the Web (Fidel et al. 1999). The strong objection of older teens to the use of kids' spaces in libraries suggests that it is wise to separate middle and high school homework help pages from elementary school homework help pages if you intend to appeal to your targeted users. This also permits the library to respond to the different cognitive levels of various age groups. For example, high school students reading at grade level may well be able to access technical or academic material written for adults, whereas only the most advanced elementary school students would be able to fully understand a scholarly article.

Research on youth Internet information-seeking behavior suggests the approaches to take when you design library websites:

Keep it simple. When a lot of effort is required to interpret the results of their searches, students don't use them. Fidel et al. (1999) found that older students do not scour lists of information for what they might need; Bilal (2007) found that younger students won't click on more than a link or two to find what they need. Students want to scan pages quickly to find relevant information, and they simply ignore anything that appears to be information overload. The implication for designing a homework website? Keep it simple. The Boise (Idaho) Public Library does this on its "Do Your Homework!" page, which includes the catalog, descriptions of and links to a few databases, links to a few recommended search engines, and a list of recommended websites split into grades K–6 and grades 6–12. If your library offers a much broader range of information and services that are useful for homework help, organize the links so your services are easily scanned without making your homework help pages look like overstuffed armchairs of information. For example, on the Cimarron County (Kansas) Library young adult page, a column for homework help highlights twelve subject categories in one color with associated topics in a different color so students can easily scan for the broad topic they are investigating (e.g., history) and then a more specific subject area (e.g., women's history).

Explain. When young children research online, they want help. Walter (2003) reports that as they research, students want adult confirmation that they are taking the right approach to the process. Even though they need assistance, however, when they work on their own students hardly glance at online help functions (Large 2004). Since frequently students use the Internet for homework without an adult beside them to consult, but they are not likely to press the help button, the implication is that on your web pages you should explain services to your patrons in brief, clear, age-appropriate language and include precisely how to use them. To you, a seasoned library user, the concept of "database" is clear, but a fifth grader may have no idea what that is, let alone how to access it. As an example, on the Brooklyn (New York) Public Library Homework Help page, the following appears under a link for "Databases for Kids": "A database is a site that will look through hundreds of newspapers, encyclopedias, magazines and books for you. All you have to do is type in one or more words to describe what you're looking for and then let the database do the rest." This kind of embedded assistance is important because the literature on information-seeking behavior shows that no matter what the age group of the searchers, a major obstacle to students' effective use of search mechanisms is that they just don't know how to use them.

Window dressing counts. Large (2004, 306) found that one of the things that most appeals to young researchers about web portals specifically designed for them is the use of color, graphics, and animation. The lesson here is that using what educators refer to as "visual text" can enrich the written text on your homework web pages to make them more attractive to young users and, therefore, increase the likelihood that they will use the site.

Pick and choose what you say. Quite a bit of the research on how students search the Internet points to a disconnect between students' vocabulary and facility with keyword searching and the vocabulary used in information systems (Bilal 2007, 44). Homework help websites must use vocabulary that is accessible to the users without being condescending to them, which risks their resentment. One way to accomplish this is to test it: ask your teen and youth advisory group to give you their feedback on the language you use. Further, you can coordinate the language you use with the lexicon of students' assignments. For example, in Montgomery County (Maryland), students are taught to write "ECRs" (extended constructed responses). You and I would call them essays. If the Montgomery County Public Library, which has an extensive amount of homework help information for students on its website, were to decide to post essay-writing advice on its website, students scanning this kind of assistance might skip over a link titled "Help Writing Essays" but might immediately click on "Help Writing ECRs." You have to speak the same language as your clients.

Links on Your Homework Help Web Pages and Digital Collections

A range of options exist for providing homework help via your web pages separate from and in addition to the interactive technologies discussed later in this chapter. I review them briefly in this section.

Databases

According to ALA, "the most common Internet-based service is licensed databases, which are available in 87 percent of all libraries and 98 percent of urban libraries" (ALA 2009b, 2). Just because a library has an educational database does not mean that database can be easily searched or is organized in such a way that it meets *students'* academic needs effectively. If databases are selected and organized to meet students' needs, they become one of the most significant tools a library has to offer its students. One of the valuable things a library offers that the Internet cannot is free, vetted information and licensed scholarly material.

The most common way to present databases on a homework help page is by subject. Another option is to present the database titles, which are not necessarily self-explanatory, and indicate who and how this database can provide assistance. This is what the Yukon (Canada) Public Library does on its homework help web page. For example, the link to "Access Science" is followed by "Best for: high-school level math and science homework help or basic research." Similarly, a brief description of the database contents and the link for "Daily Life Through History" is followed by "Best for: homework projects on ancient or modern countries/cultures." A third option is to organize your database selections by specific grade level and topic within that level. The main advantage of this approach is that students define their schoolwork in precisely this way: they are in x grade, doing a report for y subject. On its "Databases by Grade Level" web page, for example, Davenport (Iowa) Public Library divides links for school-relevant databases into subject within the following categories: "Primary/Elementary," "Middle School/Junior High School," "High School Level," and "College and University Level."

Make sure to provide tips on using databases and put the links where kids go on the library site. Specifically, include suggestions on how to find effective search terms. Often this requires not only vocabulary but enough knowledge of the area of research to come up with alternative terms. I once had a student who selected abortion as her topic for a persuasive essay based on scientific evidence. She had heard the topic discussed extensively and even participated in debates on the subject, but always in terms of the underlying ethics. It was very challenging for her to come up with search terms that could help her access scientific research that has been used to debate the pros and cons of legalized or government-subsidized abortion, such as "stages of fetal development," "medical impact of an abortion," and "abortion and the health of the mother."

Nahl and Harada (2004) found that students often lack sufficient background to conduct effective research. If you can coordinate your assistance with the local curricula, you will be able to suggest specific approaches for projects that can provide precisely the kind of guidance students need when they access your website for homework help. For example, if local fourth-graders always do a report on a country in Africa in the second quarter, and you know the types of information included in the assignment rubric, you can include a link for that specific assignment or type of assignment that includes suggested language for finding out, for example, the tribal groups residing in that country.

Since research shows that students do not use hyperlinks as often as one might expect, you should not make your student users travel throughout your site to find databases they need (Wallace et al. 2000). One library site I visited had a "homework help" link on the kids' page, then a link on the "homework help page" to the "databases page," then links to database subjects without differentiation by grade or age, and, finally, direct links to several databases. Too many steps were involved to find the right databases, and then, even as an adult, I wasn't sure I had found the right material for an elementary school student. Take the time to put the link to the databases students use within the first page or two they visit on your website.

Subject Guides/Pathfinders

Subject guides or pathfinders are exceptionally valuable to students doing homework. Rather than struggle to figure out which books, journals, and websites they should use to find information on, say, the history of slavery in the United States, students can go to a library website and then directly to a pathfinder. Or so it could be. All too often, this is not available for students, they don't know it is available if it is there, they can't find it, or it is not current. To be useful to students doing their homework, subject guides and pathfinders need to be accessible, presented in a way that directly ties to the curricula, and current. Again, as I have navigated homework help sites, occasionally it is easy for me to find the subject guides or pathfinders that will meet or even exceed the information needs of young patrons. On other sites, links from the kids' pages to homework pages to subjects do not include information as thorough or specific as that available for adults. For example, virtually every high school student in the country and many middle school students learn about Shakespeare and do some kind of project on him and the Elizabethan era, but several websites I visited either had no subject guides about Shakespeare or had guides that were buried in a long list of pathfinders for adults. Your young patrons would be spared time, effort, and frustration by having access to subject guides that dovetail with their research assignments. If your library provides information guides, those for students should be as comprehensive as those for adult patrons.

The large number of dead links is of particular concern. In just weeks or months some of the links you include in your subject guides may disappear. Effective subject guide maintenance requires regularly checking the links in the guides. To that end, you or your staff can test the links, or you can download commercial or free link-checking software.

Links to Trusted Websites

Students need to learn how to navigate the Internet, and librarians, as noted earlier, can help them do so by providing classes on information literacy. Until students become experts themselves, vetting links for accuracy and dependability is an exceptionally valuable service. Links might include websites that provide the following services, each of which is directly or indirectly related to homework assignments:

+ Online digital collections, such as the Internet Library (www.ipl.org) or Project Gutenberg (www.gutenberg.org)
+ Reference sites such as online dictionaries, thesauruses, and translators
+ Sites in languages spoken by your library's student population
+ Other compilations of trusted websites such as the ALSC's "Great Web Sites for Kids," which is organized by subject heading and includes a prominently displayed search feature (www.ala.org/gwstemplate.cfm?section=greatwebsites&template=/cfapps/gws/default.cfm)
+ Math instruction and practice, organized by grade level and topic
+ Writing and grammar instruction and practice, organized by general level
+ Study habits tips, compiled by your own library staff or links to outside guides
+ Online testing practice
+ Handwriting instruction and practice
+ Homework advice from outside sources, such as the U.S. Department of Education's "Homework Tips for Parents" (www.ed.gov/parents/academic/involve/homework/index.html)
+ Recommended search engines
+ Library pamphlets or handouts your library creates on homework tips

RSS Feeds

"Really simple syndication," or RSS, feeds allow computer users to keep abreast of new information that is posted on blogs or by various organizations on their websites. RSS feeds address the problem of spending too much time on various favorite websites every day to see if new information has been posted. Instead, by subscribing to a blog or website's RSS feed, you can access information in one place. Users need to use an "aggregator" or download aggregating software to decipher the code in which an RSS feed is written, but both allow users to go to a single place for all the RSS feeds to which they want to subscribe. Although RSS feeds are relative new technologies, they appear in this section about the more traditional online library services because they are one-way; through RSS feeds, like subject guides or databases, the library can deliver information to patrons, but patrons cannot edit or change that information.

Subscribers can keep up to date on information relevant to school assignments if their feeds are organized by grade or subject. For example, you can let young users know when they can come in for information literacy training and formal tutoring. One of the most promising uses of RSS feeds for students using library services for help with their homework is informing them when new books or articles that meet previously established search criteria become available. Some database vendors offer this option, too.

TWO-WAY COMMUNICATION: INTERACTIVE HOMEWORK HELP FROM REMOTE LOCATIONS

Some services that are integral elements of homework are interactive by definition, such as reference services, and they have continued to be interactive as technologies multiply. Others are fairly new to the library scene in general, and their use for providing homework help is relatively unexplored territory. These include blogs, wikis, Twitter, and social networking sites such as Facebook and MySpace.

Interactive Reference Services

The first order of business when it comes to providing homework help for students from afar is to let them use your reference services. For many decades, students have been deterred from using telephone and other reference services because some libraries, as a policy, treat students' queries differently than adult queries even if the queries themselves are identical. However, students, especially because they constitute such a large percentage of your patron population and are the lifeblood of the library, deserve the same consideration, attention, and level of service accorded to adult patrons. Also, learning to use the library's reference services is as important a part of the educational process as learning to use the encyclopedia. The purpose is the same: learning to use various resources to access information. To deny students access to some e-mail and live reference services is unfair on two counts: it is unfair to librarians because it turns them into the homework police; and it punishes all students because a few will make the unethical decision to get information from the librarian that they were supposed to look up themselves in a specified book or manner. But just as you would not deny a student access to books because she might use a quote without attribution, you should not deny a student access to telephone reference services because he might say he got the answer you gave him from a different source. Admirably, some libraries have instituted equal treatment of student and homework queries in their reference policies. For example, Morton Grove (Illinois) Public Library's reference services policy includes this statement: "Questions regarding school assignments will be treated as any other request for reference assistance."

Another deterrent to students using reference services is the tendency of some librarians to refer young patrons to a homework help chat vendor as soon as the word "homework" is uttered. Some library websites are similarly organized so that a click on the "homework" or "homework help" link goes directly to either databases, subject guides, or an online chat reference vendor specifically dedicated to tutoring students. This is bound to be frustrating for student users. Most libraries offer a range of reference services from afar, and the key to students using them effectively is to ensure that they understand the purpose of each resource, not just those resources that include "homework" in the title. When a student needs to figure out how to solve a math problem, it is probably best to refer him to an outside vendor-managed homework help chat service, such as the popular subscription services used by many states or library consortia. But if he needs to know the population of France, telephone reference is a far more efficient and appropriate service. Part of your role is to help students learn which services to use under which circumstances.

The first step to ensuring that students use remote reference services correctly is to post explanations and examples on your website. An excellent example of tailoring this kind of information to the needs and interests of students is provided on at homeworkNYC.org, a joint effort of the New York City Public, Brooklyn Public, and Queens libraries of New York City. The site includes descriptions of the type of assistance offered by the three types of live reference services these libraries provide (Ask-A-Librarian for quick telephone and e-mail reference, Dial-A-Teacher for assistance from a certified New York City teacher, and Live Homework Help for twenty-minute chat sessions with a vendor's tutor). What makes this website particularly useful to students is the quick summary of all three options on the first screen that appears when a student goes to the website, followed by more detailed information when the student scrolls down the page. If a student immediately encounters lengthy descriptions on the first screen she goes to, interest is likely to wane before she finds what she needs. If a student clicks on "Homework Help" and finds a long description of Tutor.com in front of him, even if his only question is the about the population of France, he may go to Tutor.com instead of picking up the phone.

Telephone Reference

The most crucial element of successful telephone reference for homework help is making sure students know they can ask only questions that require *brief* and *distinct* answers. Examples can be extremely helpful to model appropriate questions, especially if you have a separate page that targets student users (sample questions on pages for all library users would include questions that are irrelevant to homework and therefore might be distracting instead of illustrative). Good examples from the Wake County (North Carolina) Public Libraries telephone reference website include the following:

+ What is the capital of New Zealand?
+ What is the population of Wake County?
+ How do you spell "capitulate" and what does it mean?

King County (Washington) Public Library provides a useful, long list of sample telephone reference questions divided by subject, such as these:

+ Who said: "The only thing we have to fear is fear itself?" (Literature and Language)
+ How do you convert degrees Fahrenheit to Celsius? (Science, Math, and Medicine)
+ Which U.S. presidents died in office? (Geography, History, and Current Events)

Students should also understand in advance, via your website summary, that questions with lengthier answers may result in a callback, if your library has such as service, guidance to other resources, or the suggestion that they come to the library in person to access more detailed information. Telephone reference can be useful to students, but if they don't understand the parameters and you say you will call back, they may feel as frustrated as if you just put them on hold.

E-Mail Reference Services

E-mail reference service first began to gain in popularity during the 1990s, and many libraries continue to offer it. Some libraries offer a "live" version, but for many, patrons fill out a form that includes their question and are promised an answer within a specified period of time, usually one or two days. Most of these forms include the suggestion that the patron call if an immediate response is required or use different resources, such as coming into the library, if detailed information is needed. The Tompkins County (New York) Public Library includes these clear instructions for patrons of e-mail reference:

What We Can Do:

+ Answer simple, factual questions such as:
  Who was . . . ?
  When did . . . ?
  What is . . . ?

+ Answer your questions about the library and library services.
+ Answer simple questions about Ithaca and Tompkins County.

What We Cannot Do via the Ask-a-Librarian E-mail Service:

+ Answer lengthy or complex questions. Answer broad or vague questions.
+ Genealogical questions or research. We do offer Tompkins County Research, but not through the "Ask-a-Librarian" service.
+ Interlibrary loans.
+ Book holds or requests.

These are precisely the kind of instructions that clarify for students how best to use this type of reference service, thereby heading off unrealistic expectations at the pass.

Chat Reference Service

According to Reference and User Services Association guidelines (RUSA 2004), virtual reference can be defined as "reference service initiated electronically often in real time, where patrons employ computers or other Internet technology to communicate with reference staff without being physically present. Communication channels used frequently in virtual reference include chat, videoconferencing, Voice over IP, co-browsing, email, and instant messaging."

E-mail reference and even telephone reference qualify as "virtual reference," but more often than not the term is used to apply to forms of chat reference. Library chat reference services emerged as a response to the growth of commercial search companies, which challenged the library's role as the central resource for research information. As library consultants Steve Coffman and Linda Arret (2004) point out, "[By] the late 1990s, it had become apparent that if librarians were ever to successfully move their reference services to the Web, we needed . . . something live, interactive and real time." Some libraries began to use free or low-cost chat and IM programs; others used more elaborate software and programs with features such as co-browsing, which involves the reference librarian actually taking over a user's computer to bring up relevant web pages and other information for the patron. The concept of library chat reference was explosive. In 1999 just a few libraries offered virtual reference services. Within five years, hundreds of libraries offered some version of virtual reference.

Almost all libraries that offered chat reference services found themselves responding to questions by students seeking help with their homework. The value of chat reference to students is clear: they can get one-on-one assistance wherever they are when they sit down to do their homework. Most important of all, chat is a communication format thoroughly embraced by children of all ages. If, as many youth-sensitive librarians assert, it is important to seek out patrons where they are most comfortable rather than expect them to come to the library, then chat reference services have an extremely high potential for fulfilling the needs of young users—at least those with access to computers or Internet accessible phones. Chat reference as virtual tutoring for students blossomed at the same time as general virtual reference expanded. Online tutoring was first made available through libraries in 2000. By 2008, 181 library jurisdictions representing a thousand libraries offered web-based chat specifically tailored to schoolwork (Mediavilla 2008).

Virtual reference via web-based chat has met with mixed results. Lupien (2006) speculates that this may be because of ineffective marketing, user behavior, or technical glitches such as pop-up blockers, firewalls that prevent cobrowsing, or incompatible software. Furthermore, answering chat reference questions can take more time than a phone interaction. The cost of web-based services is also prohibitive for an individual library. To address the issue of cost, library cooperatives developed shared services, and many states have instituted statewide programs funded initially through LSTA. If a library tries to provide virtual reference services alone, costs might be double or triple the cost of using a statewide or other consortial service. Low-usage concerns can also be addressed by creating cooperatives and statewide consortia; only "a few very busy virtual reference services get thousands of questions each month," and all services are provided by large groups of libraries (Coffman and Arret 2004).

Who *is* using virtual reference? Students: "School children . . . make up a large proportion of the users of chat reference in most public libraries" (Coffman and Arret 2004). Even services that are not specifically designed to meet student needs are popular among schoolchildren. For example, Bailey-Hainer (2005) found that 50 to 53 percent of AskColorado's users are "consistently . . . K–12 users. Other statewide cooperatives have similarly high usage patterns." The question, then, is not whether to provide chat reference for students doing homework, but how. The choice is between web-based virtual reference or IM chat reference service.

Web-based homework help chat can consist of a statewide general reference consortium (e.g., AskColorado, QandANJ, NCknows, or AskAway [Illinois]), a cooperative general reference service (e.g., New York City's Ask-A-Librarian service), or homework-specific reference, which involves instruction as well as general reference services. The latter is often run by a private vendor. Homework-specific services can be especially useful if tutors are local teachers, such as the New York City teachers who provide assistance via New York

City's Dial-a-Teacher (available either online or via the telephone), the result of a partnership of three library systems and the United Federation of Teachers, the union representing the city's public school teachers. Commercial vendors such as Tutor.com, Homework Live, or Brainfuse, whose services are purchased by statewide consortia or cooperatives, are also popular. The State of California began using such companies for its constituent public libraries in the earliest days of public libraries' homework-oriented web-based chat reference. Walter and Mediavilla (2005) examined the effectiveness of these services in 2005 and found that they needed work. By 2008, when Mediavilla conducted a second evaluation, she found that two-thirds of patrons and 90 percent of libraries were satisfied with the services (Mediavilla and Walter 2008).

In recent years, IM reference chat has grown in popularity. IM is generally less formal, involves a faster connection, and is much less expensive than web-based chat unless your library has access to free or reduced-cost web-based chat through your state or local library cooperative. Furthermore, given the popularity of IM among youth, students may be more eager to take advantage of IM reference services. School libraries are beginning to recognize the pervasiveness of IM among their patrons, and they "are recognizing that their visibility as a 'contact' in IM . . . is a good way to meet their users at their point of need using a low-cost technology that students are already wildly enthusiastic about" (Hurst and Magnuson 2007).

Many of the analyses of IM versus web-based chat are not homework-help specific, but the pros and cons can be applied to homework assistance. For example, Houghton and Schmidt (2005) describe the immediate log-on and miniscule delay in IM reference "conversations" between librarian and user, whereas web-based chat initiation is more elaborate:

> A typically long entry form . . . requests information from users before connecting them with a librarian. . . . Once the entry form is complete and the user clicks on the button to connect to a librarian, there is typically a 5- to 10-second delay before the librarians staffing the service see that there is a patron waiting. After the librarian clicks on the button to pick up the patron, there is another 5- to 10-second delay before the two people are connected.

Those who prefer web-based tutoring point out that the entry form allows the tutor to be prepared to address the student's concern as soon as the connection is made rather than spend chat time finding out the same information; IM fans say it just takes too long and frustrates students who feel they have to jump through hoops to get help with their homework.

Houghton and Schmidt (2005) offer a good basic analysis of the advantages and disadvantages of IM and Web-based chat in their article "Web-based Chat vs. Instant Messaging," and Michaelson (2009) examines some differences to consider when selecting a method of web-based online tutoring chat specifically aimed to help students with homework in "Online Homework Help: Evaluating the Options." Michaelson discusses issues such as privacy, student anonymity, kinds of reports available, and customer support. A wealth of information on selecting, implementing, and evaluating virtual reference is available from ALA on Fact Sheet 19: Virtual Reference: A Selected Annotated Bibliography.[1]

Which type or combination of types of virtual reference service you choose to use for homework assistance will depend on factors such as the online habits of your target population, your budget, and the accessibility of services via a state consortium or local cooperative. One of the most important things to remember is that what you choose today may be obsolete tomorrow; technology changes so rapidly that it is crucial to keep abreast of the latest developments in both hardware and software.

Library 2.0, Blogs, Wikis, and Social Networks

On the surface, grouping Library 2.0, blogs, wikis, and social networks together is cramming too many ideas under one heading. However, each of these concepts and resources is driven by a common thread: the use of technology to create "the 4 Cs" online: conversation, community, connections, and collaboration (Levine 2006). And the 4 Cs have implications for homework help.

Library 2.0

All of the other concepts mentioned in this section and many of those mentioned in the entire chapter are encompassed in the Library 2.0 philosophy—an increasingly popular approach to technology and library service. It is impossible to have a discussion about technology in library service today without addressing this idea's existence and potential—and how controversial it has become.

Library 2.0 grew out of the application of the "Web 2.0" concepts and technologies to information services. The technologies employed include RSS, wikis, blogs, podcasting, media streaming, social networks, Twitter, and more, and the approach is touted for "the level of integration and interoperability that is designed into the interface through your portal" (Abram 2006). To its advocates, Library 2.0 provides the opportunity to reach clients where and how they choose to access information, to connect users with each other through technology, and to encourage users to create content, thus actively participating in the library experience. A major emphasis is "perpetual beta"—constant change as users create and tweak content. One way of implementing Library 2.0 is described by University of Houston technology librarian Karen Coombs (2007); she and her staff combine different technologies but give them a "common look" so that patrons can recognize the connection to the library as they participate in the technology.

Others feel that the ideas defined as unique to Library 2.0 are actually concepts that have always been intrinsic to innovative library service; now they are just going by a different name. Some feel that by renaming and claiming these concepts for their own, Library 2.0 advocates diminish the accomplishments of pre–Library 2.0 groundbreakers. As *LibraryStuff* blogger Steven Cohen (2006) points out:

> L2 as a concept is nothing new. "Making the library user centered": Not new. "Encouraging user participation": Not new. "Feedback in developing library services": Not new. "The user as a participant, co-creator, builder and consultant": Not new.

It is true that many of the ideologies underlying Library 2.0 have been fully supported in libraries over decades and have been responsible for valuable innovations. However, Library 2.0 diverges from the past with its emphasis on encouraging patrons to use a plethora of tools that are barely out of their infancy to accelerate two-way communication between library and patron and patron and community. Each year, it seems, new technologies that facilitate communication explode on the scene.

Another difference between Library 2.0 and other resources and innovations is worth mentioning: Library 2.0 advocates the use of technologies with which the patron may be more familiar than the librarian, specifically younger patrons who gravitate without hesitation toward new technologies, becoming expert in them while many adults are still trying to read the manuals.

If you welcome new information and communication technologies, if you are interested in learning how they can improve your services and engage your users, it matters little whether you think in a philosophically cohesive way about expanding interactive technologies under the heading "Library 2.0" or choose to discuss each new interactive technology on its own merits without ever uttering that phrase. In both cases, the potential for new technologies such as wikis, blogs, and social networks to impact homework help via the library should not be ignored, even though these mechanisms have not yet been developed for this purpose.

Wikis

Most of us are familiar with the expansive online, user-created encyclopedia Wikipedia; fewer of us realize that Wikipedia is just one example of a wiki. Augar et al. (2004) give a quick outline of the who-what-where-and-how of using wikis in which they pin down this elusive definition:

> Wikis are fully editable websites; any user can read or add content to a wiki site. . . . Users can visit, read, re-organise and update the structure and content of a wiki as they see fit. This functionality is called *open editing.* . . . All a user needs to edit and read a wiki is a web browser.

Wikis can be open to the entire public, like Wikipedia, or private and limited to a particular group of members. Libraries across the country have begun to use wikis to facilitate readers posting reviews of books and to create subject guides or pathfinders to which experts and knowledgeable patrons can contribute. Private wikis can be valuable in education as well because they can facilitate online discussion, collaborative work, and group writing projects. It is these same qualities that make wikis useful for homework help. Librarians can help students set up wikis to work on collaborative homework projects with their classmates, and a youth librarian who knows that a particular unit is under way in local schools can work with teachers to create a private wiki for students enrolled in the relevant classes to share their experience and resources.

Blogs

The Internet contains millions and millions of blogs. So who needs another one? Blogs are a tool to keep your patrons involved in your library. Blogs can be used to post announcements and to provide homework help. If you can create a blog that is tied into local school curricula, you can remind young patrons of upcoming projects or assignments for which the library offers useful resources. Young adult librarian Sarah Cofer of Northwest Library (Ohio) enlisted teens to help design her young adult blog, where she posts and some teen fans regularly reply to announcements and blog posts. According to Cofer, this "blog is usually the 2nd or 3rd most viewed section of our entire library" (Manney 2009).

At the same time as libraries are increasingly using blogs for announcements and feedback, teachers are examining ways to incorporate blogs into education. English teacher Stacy Kitsis uses blogging regularly with her students to turn homework into dialogue by posting questions related to texts students are reading (Kitsis 2008, 33). Librarians can learn from this example by exploring the potential of initiating dialogue among patrons via blogs dedicated to specific grade levels and subjects or by working with teachers in nearby schools to jointly enhance homework help with blogging.

Social Networking

Though blogging is a form of social networking, the two most famous networks used by students are Facebook and MySpace. Kids use these networks to make public comments to their friends about anything from the mundane to the important. They upload photos and drawings, and they subscribe to various causes and post virtual bumper stickers to announce their beliefs. The introduction of these social networks is profound. As one example, just a few years ago colleges assigned freshmen roommates to incoming students, and roommates met for the first time when they showed up for orientation week; now at many colleges incoming students select their roommates via social networks, and frequently kids go off to college for the first time having already established Facebook or MySpace friendships with their new classmates. Recognizing the import of social networks to young people, many organizations, including libraries, are beginning to create Facebook and MySpace pages through which they can reach out to younger patrons. The Denver (Colorado) Public Library, for example, has created eVolver, a MySpace page for the teen programs. The MySpace page includes announcements, but it also has links to various homework resources, including databases and the AskColorado reference service. Another example of a youth services social networking site is Allen County (Indiana) Public Library's children's services Facebook page, where events in the library and community are announced, books are discussed, and the fans of the page appear to be active posters on the library's "wall." Adding links to homework resources and discussions about types of homework assignments can expand the page's role to provide homework assistance as well as information about the library and community.

* * *

In a recent *New York Times* article about an Arizona high school that uses computers instead of textbooks and broadcasts podcasts of teachers' lectures, the Calcasieu Parish school system's chief technology officer, Sheryl Abshire, comments, "Kids are wired differently these days. . . . They're digitally nimble" (Lewin 2009). If libraries are to respond effectively to the homework help needs of these digitally nimble students, they must keep up to date with technology in library buildings and through the Internet. This means creating websites with homework help sections that reflect the search behavior of youth, so that the kids are more likely to use the sites and, when they do, are more likely to find information efficiently. It means examining virtual reference services so that your library utilizes a format likely to appeal to young patrons and meet their needs. It means keeping current with new communication technologies, such as wikis and blogs, and figuring out how they can be used to enhance homework assistance for your patrons. It means "hanging out" on the same Internet street corners—like Facebook and MySpace—as your patrons and figuring out ways these networks can support your patrons' educational goals. When it comes to technology, you need to find out how—within your budget, staff, and space constraints—your library's homework help program can be as cutting edge as possible.

Note

1. ALA Library Factsheet 19: "Virtual Reference: A Selected Annotated Bibliography," www.ala.org/ala/professionalresources/libfactsheets/alalibraryfactsheet19.cfm.

SIX

Answering Homework Queries and Interacting with Students

W HEN A LIBRARIAN or library staff member helps a student with a homework assignment, that librarian becomes a teacher. Under some circumstances, the librarian's role as teacher is formal; in some school systems, the school librarian or media specialist implements a lesson plan with all students to teach them to access databases, use the catalog, or conduct research. More often than not, though, the connection between information services and education is not quite so precise, even within school buildings and youth services areas of public libraries. No class in school is called "How to Access, Examine, and Evaluate Information for Use while Doing Your Homework." No grades in the subject affect a student's GPA. No standardized tests are administered to be sure our children are learning it well. But make no mistake about it: every time you help a student with a homework assignment, you are teaching that student how to navigate the world of information and, in the very essence of the word, you are a teacher.

Like all teachers, librarians can improve their services if they use successful pedagogical practices. In this chapter I investigate which pedagogical practices can inform homework help in libraries. Effective pedagogy requires effective "instructional strategies, management techniques, and curriculum design" (Marzano et al. 2001, 10). Librarians usually cannot influence educational management techniques or the curriculum in schools, but they can utilize effective instructional strategies. Many already do so.

The first important point to recognize is that as individual teachers you *can* make a difference. Over and over again studies have shown that students are influenced by and respond to individuals. Your collection is complete, your technology is cutting edge, your youth services areas are designed to accommodate youth preferences, and your web pages are perfectly organized with exceptional graphics. Yet without individuals who can help your patrons utilize the services you provide and access the information you house, your homework help menu of services can never reach its full potential.

Themes that run throughout research in education and form the nexus of recommended pedagogical practice involve classrooms becoming more student centered, just as information services are becoming increasingly more user centered. In education, this means the teacher is no longer omniscient, imparting knowledge to unenlightened students. Instead, the emphasis is a partnership between teachers and students in the learning process, with teachers serving as guides. Techniques include creating a welcoming environment in which students are most likely and able to be receptive to learning, relating what students learn to real life, emphasizing the value of the thinking process over memorizing facts, being aware of and responsive to different learning styles, and using effective praise and feedback to encourage and guide students. These techniques can be just as effective in the information services environment as you work with students to support their academics and improve literacy. When you help students learn to navigate the Internet or access your collections, examples you use to illustrate information literacy skills should relate to students' real lives. You are not just providing information to your patrons; you want them to learn the process to access that information so eventually they will be able to do so without your assistance. To maximize students' library learning experiences, librarians should be aware of different learning styles and use praise effectively to give students effective feedback about the information retrieval process.

CREATING AN ENVIRONMENT CONDUCIVE TO LEARNING

The implications that emerge from education research and teachers' practical experience about creating an environment in which students are most receptive to learning are simple and boil down to this: be kind, be aware, be understanding, and follow the golden rule.

Make Kids Feel Welcome

The first thing you need to do to make kids feel welcome is to like them. It is not especially surprising to find "pedophobia" or "ephebiaphobia"—fear and dislike of children and teenagers, respectively—on a list of phobias. It *is* surprising to find that these conditions exist among some who work with young people, including teachers and librarians: "It is amazing that there are teachers who do not like young people. These teachers typically love their subjects, but they consider students to be a necessary annoyance factor" (Kelly 2004, 275). Students are especially sensitive to adult antipathy toward them, even antipathy an adult tries hard to bury. You really cannot make students feel welcome unless, underneath it all, you like kids.

One of the best approaches to make students feel welcome is the golden rule: treat your patrons as you liked to be treated when you were their age. Remember what it was like to be young and going to the library for your school assignments. Try to recall what it felt like to encounter adults who were kind and responsive, or those who were harsh and insensitive. If you find youth culture alien and repugnant, remember that many adults disapproved of your generation's choices of hairstyle, clothing, or slang and even belittled the values your generation held dear. With this in mind, try to look beyond any aspects of youth culture that feel uncomfortable to you in order to let empathy, not ambivalence, inform your interactions with students.

A corollary to invoking the golden rule is to make kids feel that they matter. If you use eye contact when you talk to them, rather than look at your computer or papers on your desk, students feel you are approachable and attentive to their concerns. Circulate among them and ask them questions that show interest in them as people in addition to asking them about their work; this helps create personal connections. Many librarians also recognize the importance of welcoming students with warmth and personal connections. In a classroom or school media center, teachers and librarians can develop personal connections through consistent contact with a set group of students. In the library you cannot do that, though you may have regulars who frequent your building after school to do their homework. Still, you can welcome your young patrons, learn about them, and find out who they are to show them they are important in your building.

Understand How Kids React to Adults

Every teacher knows that students' radar regarding adults is honed and ready. They instantly detect whether you are in an upbeat mood or having a bad day.

They notice you changed your hairstyle or glasses before your family remarks upon it. They watch you very, very carefully. Students may not spend all day five days a week in your library watching how you behave as they do with their teachers, but you are an authority figure involved with their education, an adult in the know. As such, you should be prepared for similar scrutiny that affects how they react to you. First impressions matter quite a bit to students. They wait to see how you act, and then their "judgement is very quick and often very accurate. Students are experts at telling which teachers are pushovers and which are not" (Kelly 2004, 10).

Honesty from adults is important to students. If you do not know the answer to a student's question, you should admit it rather than hide it. This advice appears throughout educational literature and applies to library interactions, too. Students need to know that you won't bluff and that they can trust what you tell them. The twentieth-century psychologist Eric Erikson found trust in adults was especially important for younger children. Also, in a student-centered youth or teen services area, admitting you don't know the answer forms not only the basis for trust between you and your patron but also the opportunity to invite the patron to join you as a partner in the search process for the answer to the question.

Along the same lines, when students hear an adult use stereotypes, they tend to question the veracity of the rest of what that adult might have to offer. Of course, we are all aware that demeaning stereotypes of any kind have no place in the library, but sometimes we unwittingly invoke stereotypes in an attempt to be empathetic, which can backfire. If you tell a struggling seventh grader not to worry because "all middle schoolers have trouble concentrating on questions like this," your listener may well know classmates whose concentration skills are exemplary, and your credibility is destroyed.

Research in education shows that students respond best to warmth from adults and prefer to be involved in dialogues with them rather than to be lectured by them (Glasgow et al. 2006). If students are uncomfortable with the person who has the information they need, the "social dimension" alone may be enough to prevent them from trying to access that information (Shenton 2007). Similarly, when you are working with students in the library, how comfortable they feel with you may be the determining factor in how much help you can offer them.

Understand and Be Sensitive to the Population You Serve

Who are these young people coming into your library or going to your website for homework help? To provide the most effective homework help possible, you need to be able to answer this question and keep their qualities in mind as you interact with them.

Current statistics are available for a comprehensive description of the U.S. youth population, which is changing rapidly. The percentage of all school-age children who are of color is rapidly increasing, from 44 percent at this writing to an anticipated 50 percent by 2022. The percentage of students of Latino descent is increasingly more rapidly that any other group, and by 2015 one in four school-age children are expected to come from Hispanic households. Diverse economic circumstances and family environments influence your user population, too. Just about 20 percent of all young people under eighteen are from poor households; though this percentage rose and fell a bit each year, it has hovered around 20 percent since 1980; like most demographic factors, the number varies by race.[1] You may not have precise statistics such as these for your user population, but you should familiarize yourself with their characteristics to the extent possible in order to determine how best to be sensitive to your community's needs.

Finally, whatever the cultural, economic, family, or racial differences among your user population, about 10 percent of students are gay or lesbian, and you should anticipate that this percentage applies to your user population as well.

A buzz phrase in education today is "culturally responsive teaching," a concept that is equally important when you help students with their homework in the library. The basic idea is to welcome and be responsive to diversity. Glasgow et al. (2006) recommend these research-based approaches to employ with students from diverse backgrounds:

+ Develop "multicultural competence," an understanding and appreciation of diverse cultures.
+ As you speak with students, consider whether anything you say or any example you use might make students of particular religious, racial, ethnic, economic, or cultural backgrounds feel insulted or uncomfortable. If you think there is an outside chance that your language will have that result, don't use it—even if no students from the particular background in question is in the room. The same applies to sensitivity about gay or lesbian students, or those being raised in gay, lesbian, or transgender households.
+ When teachers decorate classrooms (and you decorate your youth services area), use images that reflect the diversity of the populations you serve.

Developing a solid understanding of the cultural norms in your community that affect how students learn and interact with adults is crucial to facilitate the most effective communication between you and those students. For example, if a student refuses to look at you while you describe how to use a database, you may be put off, interpreting the behavior as rude and inattentive because according to the dominant cultural norm in this country we show respect to those speaking by looking directly at them. But perhaps your community is home to students from certain Asian or South American cultures where respect is demonstrated by looking down when someone is speaking. For students from these cultures, looking directly at you would be an insult to you. Similarly, our dominant pedagogical approach focuses on having students learn by doing, discover through trial and error, and make the best effort they can. In some cultures, however, such as the Pueblo or Oglala Sioux tribes described by veteran teacher Terese Fayden (2005), children learn via extensive observation and are not supposed to try their hand at a skill until they are certain they can perform it successfully. Insisting that a Pueblo student try a computer search herself before she is ready to do so may go against everything she has learned about appropriate behavior.

Welcoming diversity also means leaving your assumptions about others' backgrounds outside the library door. Nothing reminds a student of how different he is from the majority quite like being asked what he got for Christmas when his family doesn't celebrate that holiday, thus turning a casual effort to make a personal connection into an experience that emphasizes the lack of a basis on which to build such a connection. Similarly, I watched a student squirm when a teacher assigned students the task of asking a family member or guardian a particular question about a bygone era. The teacher thought she was being sensitive by not specifying "father," "mother," or "grandparent." In fact, the squirming student resided in a homeless shelter for teenage boys; he had no relationship with anyone in his family or a guardian at that time. Obviously, you cannot be expected to know in advance every circumstance affecting the lives of your user population, but you should, at the very least, be aware that your patrons may not share the majority's religion, family configuration, or cultural background.

Be Aware of and Sensitive to Problems Students Have Finding Library Materials

Extensive research has been conducted on why and how students find information in the library and what about the way they search for information might create impediments for them, specifically as regards digital materials.

Some problems students have in the library can easily be anticipated. Younger students often have more difficulty evaluating material than older students and require more guidance. Some of the youngest students may not even know where to begin looking for information and may have no experience at all with catalogs or computers. Other differences researchers have observed are less intuitively obvious. For example, research indicates that youths avoid planning how to find what they need to know; they prefer browsing to organizing (Bilal 2007). However, they are likely to get the most bang out of their search buck if they create some kind of plan of attack, something you can help them do when you respond to their requests for assistance. Another study found that sixth graders enthusiastically conduct searches but most of the time they hardly look at the results (Bilal 2004). Knowing this, as you help students conduct searches you can demonstrate how to examine results pages effectively to extract the useful information. Similarly, Kafai and Bates (1997) found that children of all ages are disinclined to look at text-only sites; if you are prepared in advance, you can either decide to skip text-only sites as you help your patrons, or you can acknowledge that text-only might be unappealing on the surface but demonstrate that sometimes these sites contain valuable information.

Shenton (2007) outlines four "dimensions" that contribute to students' failure to find the information they need: the source dimension (the available sources are insufficient), the skills dimension (the user doesn't know how to find the available information), the social dimension (see above), and the psychological dimension (the student is too overwhelmed to even try). If you remain aware of these dimensions and collect a trove of techniques to address these problems, you can help students jump the hurdles that make accessing information in the library seem daunting.

Have High Standards for Your Patrons: Teach Them That Effort Makes a Difference

Every teacher has observed this refrain in pedagogical literature and in speeches by politicians and administrators: have high expectations for your students; expect them to do well and they will. There is, however, a big difference between having high standards for your patrons and adopting expectations that are so formidable that students are unlikely to reach them. Kelly (2004, 27) points out that "students who are the worst hurt by impossible expectations are those of low ability and low achievement. Many of these students already have self-esteem problems. However, these students' self-esteem can benefit greatly from high, yet attainable, expectations." Not all students are capable of achieving the same accomplishments, but all are capable of having goals they find challenging without getting frustrated. As you interact with students and help them attack particularly difficult assignments, you can help them break down assignments into challenging but accessible chunks so they can meet the task at hand.

Positive Attitude Counts

The flip side of the "social dimension" of information search failures is to be approachable, and this means exuding a positive attitude. Positive attitude is included in virtually every pamphlet, article, or book about how to be a good teacher, whether the advice is anecdotal or empirically based. Smile. Be kind. Encourage your charges. Let students know they can learn what you are teaching them and they will succeed. The same advice holds true for librarians working with students after school. But you are human. You will have bad days, and sometimes the needs of the students will seem overwhelming. Thompson (1998, 202) has this advice for teachers to run an attitude check and help keep their perspective on the services they provide:

+ Laugh at your problems.
+ Remind yourself that even the worst child in your class deserves the best from you.
+ Focus on the positive.
+ Be aware of the messages your body language sends. Make eye contact and smile.

SPECIFIC EDUCATIONAL STRATEGIES TO FACILITATE LEARNING

Before they become certified in their subjects, teachers are required to take "methods" courses; that is, they learn specifically how to implement pedagogical techniques in the classroom. Critical differences between the classroom and the library experience render some of the most highly acclaimed, successful education methods irrelevant to helping students with their homework in libraries. For example "cooperative learning," when students work together on a project, has been heralded as one of the most potentially powerful teaching methods available. In the library you might encourage students with similar assignments to work together, but you do not define the goals and you do not have the authority to require the students who come to your library for help to work together. Still, there are educational methods that can inform your interactions, methods that some youth librarians already utilize. You can start the conversation with open questions, listen carefully to what the student is telling you and respond constructively, help the student devise a method to address the question, model the process, relate the material to the student's life, include strategies that appeal to different learning styles, help students with study skills, and use specific techniques with English-language learners.

Ask Open-Ended Questions to Start the Conversation

Closed questions have simple, succinct answers. *What color is the sky?* Blue. *Do you have homework today?* Yes. Such questions elicit factual information, but not much elaboration. Open-ended questions, on the other hand, elicit more detailed information that can provide the basis for further discussion. *What did you learn in English today?* We read the prologue to *Romeo and Juliet.* The prologue is a sonnet. *What is a sonnet?* It's a poem with fourteen lines in a certain rhyming pattern. Shakespeare wrote lots of sonnets, mostly about love. He always rhymes his sonnets like this: ABAB, CDCD, EFEF, GG. But some other writers use a different rhyming pattern for their sonnets. *What is the Romeo and Juliet prologue sonnet about?* Shakespeare tells the audience what's going to happen—the lovers will die—and how long the play is going to last—two hours.

Ask open-ended questions to engage your clients. This is especially important when you approach students doing homework. Ask them the closed "May I help you?" and successful students will say "No, thanks" because they are sure they can do it themselves, shy students will say "No, thanks" because they prefer not to talk with strangers about their work, and struggling students will say "No, thanks" because they are embarrassed that they don't know what to do. You can probably provide useful advice for each of these types of students, but to do so you need to ask open-ended questions that lead them to tell you more. Here are a few open-ended questions that can start and enhance your dialogue with students. Remember to begin with a greeting and a positive remark (e.g., "Nice to see you today").

+ "What brings you to the library today?"
+ "I see you're looking at the [fill in the blank] books."
+ "What are you working on today?"
+ "What homework assignments do you have today?"
+ "What kinds of things do you need to find out?"
+ "What special instructions did your teacher give you about where to find the information you need?" (i.e., should the student use specific resources)
+ "Can you tell me more about your assignment or topic?"
+ "What information have you found so far?"

When you are asking open-ended questions to clarify what the student needs to know or do, ask only one question at a time. Students often either shut down when faced with multiple questions at once or select only one question of the many to answer.

Use Active Listening Skills

To some extent, the entire information services field is based on the assumption that people know how to ask questions and librarians know how to hear them and respond to them. Neither assumption is necessarily correct, especially when we are working with children who are in the learning stages of formulating queries; they may struggle more than adults with how to articulate their thoughts and ideas. Connor (1990, 52) notes that children sometimes ask for general information when what they want is very specific, an observation supported by research on the process of questioning.

"Active listening" to help students articulate their homework help needs more effectively involves listening to what the students says, repeating what the student says in your own words to be sure you understood, encouraging the student to correct any mistakes you made while you were listening, and interpreting or extending what the student says to home in on what he needs. Here is an example that might be applicable to the library:

> **Librarian:** What can I help you with today?
>
> **Student:** I have to pick a topic for my science report.
>
> **Librarian.** OK. You have a report due for your science class, and you need to decide what to write about.
>
> **Student:** Yeah, I wanted to write about Thomas Alva Edison or Alexander Graham Bell, but they were taken already when the list got to me.
>
> **Librarian:** It sounds like you have to write about inventors, but the two you were interested in were assigned to other students.
>
> **Student:** The only two inventors left when the list got to me were some guys named Nikola Tesla and Thomas Adams. I have to pick between them, but I never heard of them so I don't know how to choose.
>
> **Librarian:** If you could find out what Nikola Tesla invented and what Thomas Adams invented, you could pick your topic.
>
> **Student:** Exactly! I need to know what each of them invented.

This example illustrates another point: even though many librarians tell students they cannot help them select topics for a paper, sometimes you *can* help a student find the information that will facilitate the decision-making process, but you won't know that unless you listen to what the student has to say about the assignment.

Active listening also welcomes student questions. Students may withhold their questions for reasons ranging from self-esteem issues to not wanting to bother the teacher. Active listening shows students you are interested in their needs, that you are listening to them and encouraging them. When you do, they will be less inhibited about asking you questions.

Silence is another tool at your disposal. Most people, including teachers and librarians, are uncomfortable with silence. They try to fill it, asking another question, making a comment, or moving on to someone else to avoid embarrassment. However, research has shown that waiting for a few seconds after asking a question gives students time to gather their thoughts before answering. If you insert another question too quickly—thinking perhaps the student did not understand what you were asking or does not know the answer—instead of clarifying the student's needs, you might be denying them.

Use Process Strategies to Help Students Devise a Method to Address Their Questions

Students are patrons like everyone else; when they approach you with a question, they deserve an answer, just as you would give adults answers to queries they pose to you. When faced with a basic reference question, you should give students the appropriate answer. On the other hand, you do not want to do students' homework for them. To provide the answer without doing the work for students, show them how to use metacognitive processes to approach their assignments. Several of these strategies, especially those that are useful to students while they read, are outlined in chapter 1. A few additional techniques are described in this section.

Chunking

Chunking, a popular pedagogical technique used especially but not only with struggling students, means breaking a larger assignment or concept into smaller pieces that are more easily understood or mastered. After each "chunk," you check for understanding before proceeding to the next "chunk." For example, if a student comes to the library overwhelmed that she has to write a report, you can ask questions and make suggestions that help her delineate the tasks ahead: pick a topic, find out the information the teacher wants the report to include, organize the report into sections (e.g., background, main issue, questions to be answered, discussion, conclusion), write an outline, and so on. You can also approach the tasks at hand from different angles to help the student think about how to break down the assignment. For example, if a student needs to know why the United States entered World War II, rather than simply repeating the assignment to be sure you understand it correctly you can chunk to examine it—such as suggesting that the student find out exactly when the country entered the war, what events led up to entering the war, or what the president and lawmakers said about it at the time.

Guided Instruction, Cues, and Questions

This is really an extension of chunking. When you discuss assignments with students, give them hints and ideas for approaching the task instead of saying, "Do this." You guide by "strategically [using] prompts, cues, and questions to get the students to do more of the work" (Fisher and Frey 2008, 41). The students take the majority of the responsibility for the learning process, while you prod and choreograph to facilitate learning. Using dialogue rather than lecturing is instrumental to the success of this approach.

To help students figure out what they need to do to address assignments, Marzano et al. (2001) recommend encouraging them to set goals that are closely aligned with the teacher's goals. In the library, you can incorporate this approach by asking students questions such as "What do you think the teacher wants you to get out of this assignment?" and "What goals can we set for you here in the library so that happens?" In addition to exploring various aspects of the assignment, you can use guided instruction to help students choose which steps to take first. As with chunking, always make sure you guide the student toward sets of smaller, short-term, attainable goals so the student achieves success along the way. For example, the student who needs to pick an inventor for his science paper might divide his tasks into smaller goals: find out what Nikola Tesla invented; find out what Thomas Adams invented; pick which invention interests him the most; write a couple of sentences for the teacher telling her which inventor he will study and what he invented. Once you get students settled with an appropriate source of information, they can check off each goal as it is attained, which can guide them through the process.

Marzano et al. (2001, 113) also remind teachers that it is important to keep your charges' attention on the information they need to do their work rather than on irrelevant but interesting facts. This point can be illustrated with our example of the student choosing an inventor. In the 2006 movie *The Prestige,* a fictional Nikola Tesla based on the real inventor creates a machine to zap matter from one spot to another. Interesting sidebar, but this information is irrelevant to the student's task at hand, and raising it uses up your valuable time with the student and distracts him from his work.

Problem-Solving Techniques

As you work with students, you may find you see the same kinds of struggles over and over. You can be prepared to assist them by distributing copies of tips for specific kinds of assignments as appropriate. For example, students who are required to summarize material they read or have trouble recalling what they have read may benefit from utilizing the summarizing technique developed by Ann Brown, Joseph Campione, and Jeanne Day, which is used in many schools today. The technique involves four steps, summarized by Marzano (2001, 32) as follows:

1. Taking out all material that is unnecessary to understanding.

2. Taking out anything that repeats something you read before.

3. Using general terms instead of specific terms (e.g., "furniture" instead of "table" and "chair," or "vegetables" instead of "carrots" and "celery").

4. Picking or making up a title.

Similarly, if students need to solve a problem, you can discuss a process to accomplish that. Suggest that the student consider what she is trying to accomplish, things that prevent her from achieving that goal, and ways those things might be addressed to achieve the solution.

As you share techniques with students that can help them with their work, always remember to keep the language appropriate to the age group. For example, a nine-year-old's eyes might glaze over if you suggest that she "describe what prevents her from achieving her goal," but the concept is not a difficult one. She is more likely to understand what you are trying to communicate if you say something more like, "What things are getting in your way so you can't do that?"

Processes Responsive to Specific Learning Styles

Sometimes you can help students with their homework simply by suggesting alternative approaches that are consistent with their learning styles. Obviously you cannot administer and interpret questionnaires, called "learning style inventories," to determine every student's preferred learning style, but you can ask students if they remember things best when the teacher says them (auditory learners), or when they see them on the blackboard or in a picture (visual learners), or when they write them down themselves or act out something from the text (kinesthetic learners). You can ask students whether they prefer to listen to you describe how to do something (auditory) or to look at the directions themselves (visual). If your questions reveal that a student is likely an auditory learner and his attention wanders while he reads, you can suggest going to the audiobooks section so that he can both listen and read the story at the same time, or, if there is a space to do so quietly, you can suggest that he read it aloud to himself. For a visual learner, you can suggest she use graphic organizers for the material she is supposed to learn, and a kinesthetic learner can take notes or draw pictures to solidify comprehension.

Scaffolding

To some extent, all of the processes discussed and recommended in this chapter are examples of an effective pedagogical tool, scaffolding: "providing students with temporary support until they can perform tasks on their own" (Glasgow et al. 2006, 56). Thus, when you help a student break down an assignment into its various parts, you are creating a scaffold—a method for approaching problems—that the student can employ deliberately until she begins to do so naturally on her own each time she receives an assignment. Similarly, providing students with reading response "writing prompts" for assigned reading, such as "After I read this I wondered . . ." or "I predict the main character will . . . ," gives them a framework within which to begin analyzing the text; eventually, the hope is that the scaffold—the prompts—can be removed, but the students will still think about the text in a similar manner on their own.

Text and graphic organizers are common scaffolding tools, and you might consider creating some to use as you circulate through the youth services area and encounter students who could benefit from this kind of structure as they work. Tileston (2004) notes that, if students are trying to understand any sequence of events, linguistic organizers are especially useful. For example, you might have copies of a blank outline to give students to record the structure of a report they need to write or take notes as they read, or you might give out a "hamburger model" to help young students organize ideas for an essay. The "hamburger model," often used with very young students, consists of a stylized drawing of a hamburger in a bun from a side view. The student writes a topic sentence in the top of the bun, the main idea as the burger, and the conclusion in the bottom bun; everything else—the lettuce, pickles, sauce, cheese—are the details that support the main idea and make it "taste good." This and several other graphic organizers you might consider keeping on hand for your patrons appear in appendix B.

Model Metacognitive Processes: "Think-Alouds"

Researcher after researcher in education emphasizes the importance in pedagogy of modeling the processes you want students to use and master. The processes are metacognitive, that is, they are designed to help students think and analyze. The basic concept is the same as the message in the old adage that when you give a man a fish, you feed him for a day, but when you teach a man to fish, you feed him for a lifetime. By modeling metacognitive processes, you teach students to think for a lifetime instead of simply handing them answers for the day. "Think-alouds" (also called "self-questioning" or "self-talk") are particularly useful ways to model metacognitive academic and information literacy skills.

In the classroom, teachers conduct think-alouds and then the students, in turn, do the same. The basic premise is to speak aloud what you are thinking as you attack a problem or go through an exercise. When students begin their own think-alouds as they read or do a problem, the teacher can observe the strategies they use to analyze the text. You are not in the same position as a classroom teacher; you cannot insist that the students with whom you work walk through their thinking processes with you. But you *can* use think-alouds to illustrate skills, such as using a database, and when students try their own hand at these skills you can suggest that it is helpful for you to hear what they are thinking—and doing so, you can see if they have it down pat. You can follow up with questions to encourage think-alouds such as "What are you doing now?" or "Does that make sense to you?" or "What information have you learned so far?" The following prompts, designed for use while reading, give you an idea of the kind of phrasing that is especially useful as you model think-alouds:

+ "When I did this, I thought about . . ."
+ "I wonder why he/she/they . . ."
+ "I predict that . . ."
+ "The things I've learned so far are . . ."
+ "I want to know why . . ."
+ "Now I understand why . . ."
+ "I find that interesting because . . ."
+ "This reminds me of . . ."
+ "I want to know more about . . ."

+ "I'm confused by . . ."
+ "I'm stuck on . . ."
+ "The important thing is . . ."
+ "This is important because . . ."

The Northwest Regional Education Laboratory (2005) also publishes an online list of math think-aloud prompts, which includes these:

+ "The problem says . . ."
+ "What am I trying to solve?"
+ "The important information is . . ."
+ "The strategy I will use [to solve the problem] is . . ."
+ "Does this answer make sense?"

You can use the think-aloud method to demonstrate how to analyze or evaluate the usefulness of virtually any kind of academic text as well as skills. For example, if you are helping a student find and evaluate a social studies or science text for an assignment, you can start by discussing how you survey the text (title, picture, length, graphics), you can describe the way the contents are organized and whether the chapter titles sound useful for the student's specific assignment, and you can note section titles or unusual vocabulary. Doing this is far superior assistance than picking up a text you think will be useful to answer a query, scanning the contents, a particular chapter, and a few subheadings yourself, and then saying only, "No, this won't really help you find what you need" or "Here's the information you need for that question."

On the one hand, the idea of modeling the process sounds easy, like common sense. On the other hand, it takes less time and effort to simply hand a student a book and say, "Here, this should be useful." Often we don't think about the most basic steps we take when we tackle reading or solving a problem, so we don't share those ABCs with others. One of my most frustrating personal experiences with a new technology involved a portable recording studio. I read the instruction manual cover to cover several times but I could not understand it—I understood the words, of course, but the premise of the instructions was that the customer already knew the basics of recording music on multiple tracks; unfortunately, I was a true beginner. Your patrons may be true beginners in the process of looking for information or tackling a text for school, and one of the most helpful things you can do is show them the initial steps that will start the process rolling by demonstrating specific thinking skills, encouraging students to show you how they employ those skills, and then facilitating the internalization of those skills among your patrons.

Relate the Material to Students' Lives

Relevance is controversial. Some educators go out of their way to make their content material relevant to their students, while others are contemptuous of it. Recent pedagogical research points to its powerful impact, especially on students who otherwise struggle with academics. To be successful, making material relevant has to be designed not to tempt students to participate but rather to provide the context required to understand the material; you show them how something relates to their own experience so that students exclaim, "Oh, *now* I get it!"

In education, a language has evolved to discuss making material relevant. Students use "authentic learning materials," that is, materials they encounter in real life, and teachers might design lessons around "authentic purposes" that help students understand how the assignment makes sense in their lives. For example, an English teacher might use the Department of Motor Vehicle's handbook to teach parts of speech or grammar to high school students. Texts and assignments such as this facilitate "natural learning," that is, using real-life examples and authentic learning materials in the classroom. A similar pedagogical approach is "schema theory," which involves students tapping their "networks of knowledge, information, and experiences stored in long-term memory" to promote and enhance new learning (Roe et al. 2007, 106). One example of activating schema is starting a lesson on nutrition by hanging a large sheet of newsprint at the front of the classroom and asking students to come up and list everything they know about what kinds of foods are "good for them." Another example is handing out a list of statements to a class about whether revenge is justified and discussing them before students read Shakespeare's *Hamlet* or Euripedes' *Medea,* plays in which revenge is a major theme.

In the library you cannot implement a formal schema-activating or natural-learning lesson, but you can ask students to compare what they already know about a subject with what they are about to learn (Tileston 2004, 24). You can also build empathy by asking specific kinds of question as you discuss an assignment. For example, if a student is struggling with the scientific process, you can ask her questions about something she might have already completed using this very process without realizing it. You might ask if she has ever tried to build an igloo in the snow, reminding her that she needed to think about several building methods before deciding which to use: pat small bits of snow on top of each other, pile up snowballs, or make blocks of snow. If her choice worked, voila, she had a snow house, and next time she probably built the igloo the same way. If it collapsed, she probably tried to figure out why and chose a different method the next time.

This is not about making the material more interesting, but rather about making it more meaningful to enhance learning. You can probably pique a lot of student interest in *Romeo and Juliet* by telling ninth graders that it involves a huge party, strangers with masks on kissing each other, sex between teenagers, lying to parents, a secret marriage, two suicides, three murders, and lots of risqué jokes. But you build empathy with the characters and help students understand the social and political issues Shakespeare explores by asking them to consider how they expect to choose their mates and how they would react if their parents arranged a marriage for them, what they or others do when someone insults them or their friends, if they have ever been in or seen a fight, or what honor means to them.

Jensen (2008, 170) points out that "many learners who should do well in a subject actually underperform because the new material seems irrelevant. Unless connections are made to their prior learning, comprehension and meaning may be dramatically lessened." To pay attention to material or make the effort to understand it, some students need to know why they are learning it.

Just as teachers elicit schema to make the material relevant to their students, you can do so in the library. Even if students do not recognize any prior experience or knowledge with a subject, you can build connections for them.

Use Feedback and Praise Effectively

"The most powerful single moderator that enhances achievement is feedback . . . dollops of feedback," said education researcher and professor John Hattie in his 1999 inaugural lecture at New Zealand's University of Auckland (cited in Marzano et al. 2001, 96). At that point, Hattie had spent a decade examining thousands of studies to find out what works in pedagogy. Nahl and Harada (2004) believe feedback during the search process is just as important in library service, and Walter and Mediavilla (2005, 233) found that positive feedback was important for successful online personal interactions during reference interviews.

To improve student achievement, feedback needs to be very specific so students understand exactly what they are doing right and what they need to improve. For example, Nahl and Harada (2004) suggest assisting students conducting searches by giving them feedback on spelling, word form variations, and the breadth of the search terms. Students respond best to corrective advice when you acknowledge their successes, too, so when you need to tell a student how to improve one aspect of his work, try to praise another aspect of his work. Again, specificity makes the remarks valuable to the student. For example, you might tell a student: "Wow, you accessed that database quickly with search terms that sounded like they ought to result in a lot of articles. If you changed the search by using a synonym for . . . you'd probably find more articles to use for your report."

Part of the value of providing feedback is that it bolsters students' understanding that effort makes a difference. Researchers have found that understanding this relationship correlates more with academic achievement than learning traditional study skills (Marzano et al. 2001).

Effective praise also needs to be directed to specific accomplishments rather than reward participation or contain no useful information for the student. "Good job!" is an easy thing to say, it makes kids feel good, and it usually elicits a smile. But it does not facilitate learning. Telling a student that she added up a column of numbers well or chose a good source of information for her report is far more useful to the student. When you show a student the value of an accomplishment with praise, you also help the student make a connection for the future. For example, if you compliment a student's outline of a social studies chapter, it is helpful to the student for you to add that he can use the same kind of outline to create study notes for just about any type of humanities textbook.

In all instances in which you compliment students as you teach them literacy skills or help them with their homework, consider how they can use your positive remarks to learn more, not just feel good. On the other hand, if you think too long and hard about what you say, your remarks will lose their spontaneity and, therefore, their authenticity for students. Try to keep the educational value of praise in mind, but more than anything else keep it real.

Help Students Learn Study Skills

Part of going to school and doing homework is learning how to study. Many of the processes discussed in this chapter are study skills. Two additional study skills are worth attention because they are traditionally areas with which students have difficulty: writing and taking notes.

Students begin writing early in elementary school, where homework assignments might include writing paragraphs, journal entries, and essays as well as reports. You can, of course, direct students to reference resources to help them write, but you might consider providing writing "cheat sheets" and basic verbal instructions. The cheat sheets can include the elements of a paragraph (e.g., topic sentence, supporting detail, concluding sentence), the elements of an essay (e.g., thesis statement, supporting paragraph, conclusion), and general writing tips. They can also be written differently for different age groups or levels of language comprehension. To help students organize ideas for writing, you might create an outline designed specifically for writing a paragraph and one for writing an essay. Figure 1 is an example of the kind of organizer you can distribute to help students write a paragraph.

Taking notes on what they read is one of the most valuable study skills students can develop. Frequently students make fairly common mistakes when they take notes, and you can help them by providing them with advice, giving them a note-taking cheat sheet, or providing them with examples of good notes. The following information might be included:

+ Choose your format. You can take notes in outline form, using a graphic organizer, or both.
+ Write words or phrases, not sentences. Sentences take too much time and are harder to review.
+ Rewrite the ideas in your own words; don't copy the text exactly.
+ Underline or highlight main topics and important words to make it easier to find them when you review your notes.
+ The more you write, the better.

Special Considerations for Working with English-Language Learners

An earlier discussion centered on being sensitive and welcoming to students from diverse backgrounds. Specific tips for working with students who are learning to speak English include the following:

Speak slowly. This does not mean speaking so slowly that you sound unnatural, but try to pace yourself so the patron has a chance to decipher what you are saying.

Use simple sentence structure. The Corporation for National and Community Service recommends that member organizations instruct volunteers to "speak simply and clearly. Use short complete sentences in a normal tone of voice."[2] Remember, speaking louder does not help students understand more. Also, slang and idioms are especially difficult for English-language learners, so avoid them. For example, imagine how odd "It's raining cats and dogs" would sound to someone unfamiliar with that idiomatic expression.

Enhance discussion with visual aids. To the extent that you can do so naturally, include drawings, actions, gestures, and other alternatives to words to illustrate your point.

Avoid homonyms or words with multiple meanings. The coordinator of literacy and volunteer programs at the Jewish Community Center in Manhattan, Judy Gross, tells the story of a young English-language learner in New

FIGURE 1

SAMPLE CHEAT SHEET:
HOW TO WRITE A PARAGRAPH

WRITE A PARAGRAPH

1. Write a topic sentence. In the topic sentence, tell the reader the main idea of the paragraph. Write your main idea here in a complete sentence.

_____

_____

2. Add a concrete detail. A concrete detail is an example that supports the main idea. Write down your first example here in a complete sentence.

_____

_____

3. Comment on the concrete detail. Explain how the detail relates to the main idea. Tell the reader what you think is important about the detail. Write your comment here.

_____

_____

4. Add another concrete detail. Write down a second example that supports the main idea.

_____

_____

5. Comment on the second concrete detail. Explain how the second detail relates to the main idea. Tell the reader what you think is important about the detail. Write your comment here.

_____

_____

6. Finish with a concluding sentence. In the last sentence of the paragraph, summarize everything you wrote. Write a summary of your paragraph here.

_____

_____

_____

_____

Now write down all the sentences on a separate piece of paper to create your paragraph. Write down the sentences in order, but leave out the numbers.

York City who remained visibly confused the entire time a volunteer read him a book about a family of bunnies living on the bank of a river. The story took place in a pastoral setting, but the student thought the rabbits lived at Citibank—and, of course, that made no sense. English contains many, many words with more than one meaning and lots of homonyms. Be sure, if you use them, that your patrons understand what you mean.

Avoid the temptation to correct grammar or pronunciation. This may make students withdraw. Instead, just as the best way to teach students metacognitive processes is to model them, the best way to illustrate correct pronunciation and language structure is to model them. For example, if a student says, "I need know George Washington life," you can repeat the phrase correctly in your response: "OK. You need to know about George Washington's life. Let's look over here in the encyclopedia."

Social cues differ from culture to culture. Students may refuse to make eye contact when you speak because in their culture that is disrespectful, or they may refuse to try something you are showing them because in their culture they have learned not to try something until they are certain how to proceed. These are examples of student behavior reflecting cultural social cues rather than the dominant cultural norms of this country. Thus, don't try to force a student to look at you when you speak or assume that a student who won't try a skill you have just demonstrated is being uncooperative. Learning about the cultural cues in the groups represented in your community helps prevent these problems.

Review academic instructions and language. Essay. Debate. Evaluate. Journal. You may expect that most high school students understand these terms as well as others used in homework instructions. Some English-language learners may never have heard words such as "essay" and "journal," or they may be uncomfortable debating and evaluating because they come from countries where either political repression or cultural norms interfere with expressing what might be perceived as criticism.

Review background knowledge. Students from other cultures may not have the same life experiences as the situations depicted in the material they read for school or the same background knowledge as other students in your library. You might want to talk with students about what they already know and don't know about the topic of an assignment and provide any useful background information.

Give students a chance to gather their thoughts to answer your questions. Pausing after you ask a question is especially important with English-language learners. They need a chance to confirm for themselves that they understand what you asked and then to retrieve the right vocabulary to answer your question.

Help students with difficult and new vocabulary. Before you leave an English-language learner with a text that meets her needs, make sure she can use the text. Scan it for advanced vocabulary words or words that might be especially difficult to pronounce and review them with her.

Special Considerations for Students with Cognitive Challenges

"Special needs" is a large umbrella under which a wide range of cognitive and physical differences are categorized. Thus, the needs of special-needs students may vary widely from one patron to another. Teachers are required to follow "IEPs"—individual education plans—for all special-needs students, but librarians do not have the benefit of knowing the specific strategies that will assist their individual library users. Still, there are certain general guidelines to which you can adhere when you are working in the library with special-needs patrons who experience cognitive difficulties.

Use simple language. Special-needs students with cognitive difficulties may not be able to understand advanced vocabulary and complex concepts.

Be explicit when you give instructions. Some students may not be equipped with your underlying assumptions or understand your inferences. For example, if you are helping with a research project, say, "type the words x and y . . ." instead of "enter the phrase . . ." and specify that the student should "press the ENTER button when you're through typing."

Write down instructions. Some learning-disabled students may not be able to listen and take notes at the same time. To stave off this problem, jot down the verbal instructions you give to your special-needs patrons.

Use chunking techniques. Described earlier in this chapter, chunking techniques are especially useful for students with any cognitive disability.

Present information in careful sequence. Start with the most concrete steps and ideas and move on to abstract ideas only if the student masters the concrete ideas. For example, if you are helping a student with a simple math equation, such as 10 minus 4, you might give him ten paper clips and ask him to take away four of them and count what's left. If you are helping a student understand a story she has read, you might first discuss what the characters do or say, and when she clearly knows these details you might ask her how one or another character feels or what the character wants.

Wait for students to answer your questions. Some special-needs students struggle with communication skills. Depending on the student's special need, he may not be able to answer your questions and you may need the intervention of a parent or caregiver to help you meet that student's informational needs. However, do not presume that a few seconds of silence after a question indicates that the student cannot answer. Give him a chance before you turn to the caregiver.

Make allowances. Not only do some special-needs students look different from other students, but they may also have behavioral issues that would otherwise be categorized as misbehavior. Students with Tourette's syndrome, for example, may suddenly yell loudly or curse. Jones and Shoemaker (2001, 78) remind librarians that some of their discomfort with unusual behavior or appearance among special-education students "comes from a general discomfort with the unknown, or what is unfamiliar" and not from any threat the students pose to the library or its other users. They urge librarians to be especially patient and warm with these special-needs students.

Nip any teasing in the bud. Despite your best efforts to welcome all youth to your library, because special-needs students may look or behave differently from others, they may be ostracized or teased by nondisabled patrons. It is up to you to guard against and put an immediate stop to this behavior.

Keep high-interest/low-vocabulary collections in subjects covered by local curricula. "Hi-lo" collections relevant to the local school curricula can be of particular value to your special needs patrons as they complete their homework in your library.

A POTPOURRI OF TIPS FROM LIBRARIANS AND EDUCATORS

Some advice about interaction with students in educational settings, whether in the classroom or in the library, does not fall within the categories already covered in this chapter, but they can be valuable.

Make a copy of every assignment or reading list students bring to the library. For each assignment, write down the teacher's name, the grade level, and any resources you found to help with the assignment. Keep the assignment in a binder or file under the grade level and teacher's name so you can access it when another student comes in with the same assignment.

Create a form to send to school with students when you are unable to help them find what they need for an upcoming assignment. You can use checklists, as Connor (1990) recommends, to indicate what the student did (e.g., searched databases, searched print collection) and why the materials were unavailable (e.g., books on the topic were all checked out, no books in the collection). Students will be much less anxious about not finding what they needed because your form shows that they did try to complete the assignment.

Be flexible. This advice appears in just about every book or article about working with students. Success is being able to switch gears when something is not working. Part of the point of this chapter is to provide you with a range of approaches you can employ when you are working with students. If you are using one of them unsuccessfully, try another.

Keep your sense of humor. This is the number-one tip teachers give to each other, in offices, in lunchrooms, and in educational literature. Not only does a sense of humor help you through the rougher parts of your day, but, as Thompson (1998, 67) advises in her book on maintaining discipline among high school students, "Some teachers never laugh with their students. Don't be one of them."

✳ ✳ ✳

Cooper asks the important question "How can we move to make information in the library available to [young people] . . . and give them some control over their own intellectual development rather than force-feeding them in our attempt to nurture?" (2004, 183). This chapter is one way to answer that question: apply sound pedagogical strategies to library service to youth. Most of the strategies outlined here are fueled by a few central concepts: welcome everyone, put yourself in your patron's shoes, listen carefully, remember that the process is more important than facts, model the process, and provide useful feedback. The elements of good pedagogy parallel RUSA's five important elements of a reference interview: approachability, interest, listening, searching, and following up (RUSA 2004). Not every interaction with a young patron will or should be a "teaching moment," but each time you approach a student or one comes to you for assistance, the ensuing interchange has the potential to contribute to your patron's education in a meaningful way.

Notes

1. Statistics taken from Forum on Child and Family Statistics, "America's Children in Brief: Key National Indicators of Well-Being," 2010, www.childstats.gov/americaschildren/demo.asp.
2. Corporation for National and Community Service, "Tutoring English Language Learners," Corporation for National and Community Service Resource Center, www.nationalserviceresources.org/practices/17633.

SEVEN

Troubleshooting

The best-laid schemes o' mice an' men
Gang aft agley,
An' lea'e us nought but grief an' pain,
For promis'd joy!

—Robert Burns, from "To a Mouse"

YOUNG PEOPLE WHO come to use the library usually have no more intention of uprooting your homework help program than poet Robert Burns
had meant to destroy a mouse's home as he plowed his field. However, as Burns
explains to the frantic animal, no matter how well one plans, things go wrong.
This chapter is about some options available to you when that happens at the
library.

The number one troubleshooting tactic you have available to you is prevention. It is much easier to keep problems from developing in the first place than
to let them come to a head and then try to handle them, and it is much less
stressful to know what to do when a student approaches you with a problem
than to wing it. When preventive measures do not work, then you need a solution. In this chapter I outline both prevention and solutions for several typical
problems that arise while providing homework help to students in the library.
The problems are divided into two sections: problems relating to information
services, and behavior problems.

PROBLEMS WITH AVAILABLE INFORMATION

Too Many Students Want the Same Material

Almost all youth and school librarians have faced the situation of having many students converge on the library at the same time to conduct research for papers on the same or similar topics—papers that are due, oh, perhaps tomorrow. It is frustrating for the students and it is frustrating for the librarian. In the best of all possible worlds, you would have more than enough materials to go around. In the real world, you have a few options available to minimize this problem even if you probably will not be able to solve it altogether.

The most effective preventive approach is to work cooperatively with teachers and librarians at your local schools. If you are consistently informed about general curriculum topics each quarter during the school year for all grades, and faculty and librarians keep you in the loop when they are planning large projects, you can be prepared to meet students' homework needs when they come to the library. You can set up displays of the relevant materials and work with schools to create a reserve system for large-scale projects, similar to the type of system used in colleges, allowing students to take the books out for an hour or two. You can keep a sign-up sheet for the most-requested texts in your reserve system and call up students on the list as the books are returned. Also, a cooperative relationship with your local teachers and school administrators may help you arrange a rotating schedule when your collection for some topics does not support large numbers of students coming at once to do homework on projects in that subject area. Rotating books for any grade level is a common practice in schools when there are not enough books for every class to study the same thing at the same time. English 10 section 1, for example, completes its Shakespeare unit in the first semester, while English 10 section 2 studies *Taming of the Shrew* in the second semester. You may be able to demonstrate effectively to teachers or school administrators that students who need library resources for homework projects can benefit if the school also takes into account the library's collections when they develop unit rotations.

If student still cannot find the books they need because so many others have been to the library before them, after taking the traditional steps of checking other branches or consortia, one solution is to direct these patrons to your online collection and other web-based resources. If you plan in advance, you can keep a list of reputable websites tailored to general and specific topics within curricular areas. Also, you can refer students to your library's website if it contains these kinds of links and online collections.

Too Many Students Want Help with Their Homework at the Same Time

This corollary to "too many students want the same material" is less predictable. To prepare for a potential onslaught of students seeking your assistance, make sure you have a system in place to manage the situation. You can use a sign-in sheet similar to those used in some commercial outlets or use the "deli" approach and hand out numbers to the students. You should figure out in advance the maximum amount of time you can spend with each student when many need your help at once. Let the students know in advance they will have your attention only for x minutes because there is a line; that way, they won't be startled or feel slighted when you have to stop. Also, make sure students know up front that you can address only one concern at a time during busy periods.

Enlisting the assistance of others to handle some of your patrons' needs is another approach. With proper, temporary signage that you can post during busy times, you can divert questions to other staff or volunteers during your busiest homework help hours. Staff other than librarians can answer directional questions. As noted in chapter 4, you can recruit a group of techies from your local high school or college to answers questions about technology, a few volunteers with general expertise to help younger students, and a few volunteers with subject-specific expertise to assist older students. For example, if you regularly find students requesting assistance in math or writing, you can set aside and label a couple of tables supervised by older students or adult volunteers who can provide guidance in these areas. This frees you up to focus on reference queries and information services.

A Student Is Impatient with the Time It Takes to Find Information or Get Assistance

This is the era of fast-faster-fastest for all of us, but millennials in particular expect to get what they want instantly. Even students who have planned well in advance of due dates may seem anxious for you to respond to their needs more quickly than you can. They have usually exhausted their own resources before they approach you, whether in person, by phone, or virtually, and they expect you to be able to access your resources rapidly—in fact, that may have figured into their planning. Students who have procrastinated work on an important or long-term assignment and have exhausted their own resources are even more frustrated and pressed for time before they approach you. They may be abrupt or pushy; they may even press you to conduct searches for them.

To help prevent this, encourage your patrons to plan in advance. Colorful posters in prominent locations can urge students to plan ahead. You might be able to create a printed or online instruction booklet for how to plan for long-term projects. The first step you cover should be "calendaring" the project, that is, planning out exactly how much time to devote to each part of typical types of assignments and putting aside time to do so on a calendar that the student commits to follow. In advice you post on conducting research, include information about the role the library can play in the project, such as which materials and technology can be useful, what is and is not reasonable assistance to anticipate from a librarian, and an explanation of why it is important to come to the library early in the process of preparing for the project. Try to coordinate your suggestions with the expectations of local schools.

When you are faced with impatient patrons, the more effective approach is to be sensitive to their concerns. Radford and Connaway (2008, 10) recommend letting them "know *realistically* how long you think the search for the information they need will take. If you think it will take more than a minute or so, let them know. Present alternatives and let them decide." This may not make students any less frustrated about getting help with an assignment that is due tomorrow, but it does let them feel a little more control over the process. Let students know realistically how long you expect to take to find what they need, and let them decide if they want to wait that long. If the student does not want to wait, Radford and Connaway recommend that you apologize for being unable to offer immediate assistance and offer to e-mail an answer. Being polite and apologetic when you cannot provide what the patron wants is simply good customer service, and responding this way also helps students realize that they need to allow more time when similar assignments come along in the future.

If a student is rude to you, that is an entirely different situation, addressed later in this chapter.

BEHAVIOR PROBLEMS

Most educators agree that preventive measures are the best way to avoid behavior problems, from bad manners to disruptiveness. Educators develop class rules with the students, post them, and follow them. They vary activities so students do not become bored and restless, and they develop lesson plans based on current pedagogical theory so students remain engaged with little opportunity for acting out. Many of these generally accepted concepts in education are designed to facilitate changing the way the classroom is managed from the moment students step inside. Almost all of the activities in the classroom are controlled by teachers and administrators. The library is quite different in that student activities there are entirely voluntary. Still, some general classroom management approaches can also be implemented effectively in the library to address behavior problems. Below, various preventive techniques are described as well as specific strategies for addressing difficulties when they arise.

If you know in advance how to handle a range of unpleasant circumstances, you are more likely to remain calm and your response is more likely to be swift, fair, and effective. Furthermore, you are much less likely to get personally rattled by inappropriate behavior. It is best to start with mild interventions and ramp them up if necessary.

Establish and Post Rules and Policies Regarding Behavior

The first step to preventing issues involving behavior is to create and post rules letting your patrons know the limits of acceptable behavior. Many libraries have behavior policies for all patrons and a separate policy regulating behavior for younger people. Most are attempts to keep patrons safe, to control disruptive behavior (which is not necessarily defined specifically), or to prevent destruction of library materials. In detail, though, both the policies governing all patrons and those directed at youth vary widely. In his survey of general behavior policies, Webb (2005) found that the only universal policy was no eating, though most libraries also have a policy regarding unattended children. In much current educational literature, teachers are encouraged to ask students to help create class rules to increase the likelihood that students have a stake in following rules they help establish, a concept that grew out of the student-centered approach to education. In the library, your youth advisory group or similar representative group can help you anticipate behavior problems among their peers and design appropriate rules to ban this behavior. For many students, the fact that their peers created the rules is a deterrent in and of itself.

Once you have established rules for your library, including rules that apply to your virtual and telephone reference services if you offer them to students, the next step is to make sure students are aware of them. Post the rules prominently in several places in the youth services area. If your list of rules is too long, however, students will not read them. Though this does not mean you should not have rules covering anticipated problems, it does mean that you need to highlight the limits that are most relevant to your student population when you post them, though you might want to hang a more complete list next to the highlights. For example, if ringing cell phones are a constant irritant in your space, hang a sign asking students to turn off cell phones upon entering the library, or designate a specific area as cell phone friendly.

A list of consequences the librarian has the authority to implement should also be posted. This might range from finding and enlisting the help of the adult responsible for a misbehaving student to get his charge to behave properly to ejecting a student from the library. Some typical consequences include a warning to the student, asking the patron to leave for the remainder of the day, contacting a parent or guardian to discuss library policy and the student's infraction, and preventing access to the library facility. The Madison (Wisconsin) Public Library issues a "banning letter," which includes the specific nature of infractions that led to the expulsion, the length of time the patron is banned from library premises, a description of the appeal process, and the information that failure to cooperate with the expulsion will result in the patron being subject to arrest for trespassing. This last choice is the most serious and requires its own set of policies and documentation.

Some rules you post are really for parents, not for their children. For example, the Olathe (Kansas) Public Library informs parents: "If a child under 16 years of age is not picked up by 30 minutes after closing, and attempts to contact a parent or guardian are unsuccessful, the person-in-charge will contact the [police] to report an abandoned child." Many other libraries have similar policies.

Clear boundaries are important in all learning environments. Setting clear and consistent expectations of students' behaviors is one of the factors associated with educational resilience, that is, helping students who are at risk of academic failure due to sociological circumstances overcome those barriers. Posting the boundaries also supports librarians, who are not always perceived as authority figures by students and "seeing it in writing will help the patron recognize the validity of the policy and give the librarian credibility" (Webb 2005).

Refer to the Posted Rules

In the midst of a difficult situation, it is easy to get too flustered to refer to those rules you posted, but sometimes all a student needs to get back on task is for you to point to the list and give her a gentle, general reminder that her behavior is not permitted. If the rules were created with the cooperation of a youth advisory group, remind the student that her peers decided upon these limits.

If the disruptive or destructive behavior continues, when you warn students about potential consequences listed on your posted rules, mention only those you are willing to enforce. Otherwise students will learn that you may threaten them but you won't follow through. This compromises your authority.

Although referring to the posted rules and consequences can be effective, you should do it sparingly or you will earn the reputation among students as a martinet, effectively annulling any rapport you have built with them.

Circulate

Whenever you have the chance to do so, circulate through the youth services area with the eye of hawk but the demeanor of a lamb. This accomplishes three goals. It lets you keep an eye on the goings-on in the library; you are more likely to see a problem brewing if you are moving around instead of staying in one spot with limited visual access to the youth services area. Also, when students see you circulating, they know they are being supervised and are less likely to act out. Finally, if you keep your manner calm and pleasant while you circulate, students perceive you as approachable, and this helps build the rapport that contributes to a more cooperative atmosphere.

Monitor Students' Activities and Ask them about What They Are Doing

Showing interest in your patrons' activities builds rapport, enables you to spot students who might need your assistance before they get frustrated and off task, and encourages those who are off task to start working again.

Model the Behavior You Want to See in Your Patrons

If you want your patrons to be polite to you, be polite to them. If you want them to express their frustration in socially acceptable ways or work through their frustration rationally, show them how to do it by remaining calm and collected as you deal with difficult queries, technological glitches, or children behaving unpleasantly. To this end, treat your patrons as if they are clients. You want them to approach you showing the respect one accords to a professional with a specific area of expertise, and one of the best ways to accomplish this is to welcome them as a professional would a client.

Act Quickly

If you see disruptive behavior or a potentially difficult situation brewing, it is important to react with speed and decisiveness. It is much easier to employ a few tried-and-true behavior management techniques throughout the afternoon than to reign in a group of middle schoolers gone wild.

Encourage Students to Go Back to Work or to Library-Appropriate Activities

Even without referring to the rules, you can redirect some students simply by suggesting that they return to activities that are more suitable for the library. If you know they are there to work on assignments, you can suggest, "Why don't you finish your math homework instead of throwing your pencils across the table at each other?" If they are doing something else, you can smile as you remark, "You only have a few more minutes left on the computer before it will be someone else's turn. Maybe you'd like to take full advantage of that [instead of making phone calls]."

Pick Your Battles

Minor infractions are still infractions, but educators find that it is not terribly constructive to "call out" a student on relatively minor disruptive behavior that self-corrects, and this applies in the library as well. If a student yells across the room to a friend but then looks around sheepishly and covers his mouth, you see that he realizes his mistake and is unlikely to repeat it. Let relatively minor infractions like this slide.

Use Nonverbal Clues

Nonverbal clues can work wonders to control behavior that is beginning to stray over the line of acceptable. Catch a student's eye if she is misbehaving or seems about to misbehave and shake your head or look puzzled. Or smile at her. Sometimes this is enough to nip a problem in the bud, because the student realizes that she is not going to get away with anything. If this does not work, walk over to the student and stand near her. Frequently the proximity of a supervising adult will stop a student from bothering others or getting off task. A student has to be pretty defiant to act out directly in front of an authority figure.

Ask Misbehaving Patrons about Their Work or Activities

Asking students about their work is an effective tool to prevent misbehavior, as noted above, but it can also help you respond to misbehavior. Asking a student about what he is doing often helps bring him back on task. Remember to avoid yes/no questions, and specificity in your questions is even more important when you are responding to misbehavior. The specificity helps distract the student from inappropriate behavior and redirects his attention to your questions. Try to get a glimpse of the work in front of the student or the website on a computer so you can refer to it: "I see you have a lot of math homework there. What exactly are you working on in class?" or "It looks like you're on the Google website. Tell me about the information you're looking for." Then pay attention and respond as the student discusses what he is doing so he sees you are genuinely interested. In addition, sometimes kids get restless when they have reached a wall and need assistance to proceed. Asking about assignments may identify those who need your help.

Speak Privately with Patrons Whose Behavior Is Problematic

At a short private conference, sometimes students will take responsibility and improve their behavior when you ask them to identify ways they can cooperate. You can also provide detailed suggestions of how to approach assignments and outline the next steps in the disciplinary process if misbehavior continues to be chronic. In a private conference in the library, a student may also be more willing to admit reaching a roadblock with an assignment and needing help.

Speaking privately with students who are acting out is especially important because it allows you to discuss the problems without criticizing them in front of others. Public criticism can have the opposite effect of what you intend. In the face of what they perceive to be public humiliation, students often become silently resentful at best and belligerent at worst. They are less likely to focus on the efficacy of your concerns or consider responding cooperatively to them. An additional deleterious consequence of publicly chastising one student is the message it sends to other students. In the classroom, students tend to withdraw and hesitate to engage in class activities when they see their peers being chastised. In a library they might become reluctant to seek assistance from librarians, or they might not come to the library at all.

If you do need to speak with a student about behavior, it is more constructive to describe specific observations, such as "I noticed you grabbed Juan's book out of his hand three times so he couldn't read," as opposed to a general pronouncement about the student such as "You are obnoxious." The former statement tells the student that a specific behavior needs to change; the message of the latter statement is that the student has negative qualities—much more demoralizing problems without identifiable solutions. Similarly, the old adage that you get more with honey than with vinegar applies here as well. Students are more likely to respond if you can couch your criticisms positively, such as saying, "You and your friends will be able to concentrate better on your homework if you find a comfortable place to sit quietly" instead of "You're so busy standing around talking loudly that nobody can get any work done."

Lead a Chronic Misbehaver toward a Leadership Role

Asking a student who chronically misbehaves to take charge is counterintuitive: how can giving more attention or importance to a student who regularly makes a spectacle of himself possibly lead to better behavior? The fact is, it works. Tell a student that "I see you're looking for something else to do" and ask for help picking up books for reshelving or assistance distributing, collecting, and analyzing feedback forms. This keeps such students occupied in a constructive activity. It also can make them feel a part of the library community, which, like building rapport, helps lead to cooperation.

Remain in Control and Professional When You Respond to a Rude Student

Dealing with rude customers is often the most difficult part of any service profession workday, and the challenge is to remember that it probably has nothing whatsoever to do with you. Luckily, as Radford and Thompson (2004) point out, inappropriate reference interactions are infrequent, about 5 percent, whether the interactions involve face-to-face encounters or take place via virtual reference. Knowing that it is a relatively infrequent occurrence, however, does not make it easier to cope with when it happens to you. When it does, follow two pieces of advice often recommended to educators and librarians alike: stay calm, and don't respond in kind. This does not mean that you should not react at all. You should acknowledge that there is a problem and suggest to the student that you will talk about it with her in ten or fifteen minutes. This way, the student does not think the rudeness went unnoticed and you handle it quickly, but you get a chance to regain control so that you can discuss the situation in a constructive manner.

Second, and most important, never answer a patron's rudeness with anger or hostility. No matter how tempted you may be to do so, criticizing or snapping at a student will likely fuel rather than disperse the hostility. Not only may you find yourself in a confrontation fraught with verbal conflict, challenges to your authority, or even physical threats, but other students observing the situation will not likely be able to determine whether the student to whom you are speaking deserves the harsh treatment. What they will remember is that you were pugnacious and reproachful. The same applies to virtual interactions, where "flaming" (hostile Internet interactions) almost always exacerbates the situation (Radford and Thompson 2004). I once heard a teacher wisely observe that, no matter how supportive and warm you have been and continue to be with a student, if even once you castigate him roughly or make him feel embarrassed, *that* is what the student will always remember about you.

Understand and Prepare for Bullying

Bully victims Erik Harris and Dylan Klebold massacred twelve students and a teacher at their high school in Columbine, Colorado, in part to get revenge for bullying; on the opposite end of the spectrum, fifteen-year-old Phoebe Prince committed suicide rather than continue to face her tormentors at her high school in South Hadley, Massachusetts. Bullying is not harmless, and it should never be tolerated. Some bullying may appear to be kids joking around or minor teasing; therefore, to be safe it is best to put a stop to any repeated negative attention from one patron toward another even if it seems to be benign. Recent research shows that bullying is not only damaging to the victims, who experience a range of problems from low self-esteem to full-blown depression, but to the bullies as well. Those who have bullied others grow up to have a higher incidence of depression and criminal behavior (Crothers and Kolbert 2008). To handle this, expert advice to educators includes establishing clear guidelines prohibiting bullying and designing a plan of action for how to respond to it. Some schools, for example, have adopted programs administered by outside agencies to establish schoolwide anti-bullying programs. Your library should determine its policy on how incidents of bullying will be handled. Hiring an anti-bullying consultant may be a bit excessive or too expensive for the library, but be aware that most bullying takes place outside of formal learning environments in unstructured situations—similar to what students find at the library. At the very least, your anti-bullying policy should include making sure the victims know that the bullying is not their fault and holding a conference with the perpetrators of bullying to discuss how and why this behavior is not allowed in the library. Students who become chronic bullies should be removed from the library altogether, and the staff should consider reporting the behavior to appropriate authorities.

Handle Racism, Anti-Semitism, Ethnic Slurs, and Homophobia Immediately

Your library should also have a policy on what constitutes unacceptable behavior toward any specific racial, religious, or ethnic group and gay, lesbian, and transgender patrons, along with the range of consequences that will be applied to perpetrators of these behaviors. Perpetrators of these behaviors see them as a form of entertainment, while the victims see them as insults or, worse, emotional and physical threats—something such actions have in common with bullying. In that it is incumbent upon you to welcome all cultures within your community, you must respond when you hear students using racist, anti-Semitic, anti-ethnic, or anti-gay slurs or language.

Students will follow your lead and you should be prepared accordingly. While I was passing out papers one day, a student on the other side of the room loudly announced to two Latinas sitting near him, "Stop speaking Spanish! This is America and you should speak English!" The large, diverse class, which included students who spoke French, Spanish, Amharic, Arabic, Bengali, and a Ghanaian dialect, froze, every set of eyes on me. The tension eased only after I made clear that every language and culture is welcome in my classroom, and that the requirement to use English in my classroom is applicable only to certain kinds of assignments. Though I like to think I did an admirable job making all of my students feel welcome, I was caught entirely off guard. Since you will set the tone in your library, be prepared with how you will respond and precisely what you will say. If you ignore such insults, at best students will feel free to criticize other groups; at worst, certain groups will feel excluded from a service that is rightfully as much theirs as anyone else's.

Your policy should include publicly letting the perpetrator and victim know this offensive language is unacceptable in the library because it is hurtful to other patrons. In a private conference with an offending student, you can discuss your policy and its message in more detail, outline future consequences, and express confidence that the student will respect the rules of the library as well as other patrons of all backgrounds. Your policy might include contacting the student's parents as well. If the offender's language is physically threatening, you must contact the appropriate authorities to ensure the safety of your patrons; do not assume that you can determine whether the threat is real or all talk. As a last resort, students who refuse to respect the policy of the library to make all patrons feel welcome and safe should be banned from the premises.

Solicit Help from Others in Threatening Situations

The business of keeping patrons—and yourself—safe may go beyond employing increasingly intrusive behavior management techniques. In any workplace, if you are faced with a person who is screaming, swearing, or threatening you with physical harm, with or without a weapon, the U.S. Office of Personnel Management (1998) advises that you signal coworkers or a supervisor that you need help. If a younger student in the library is out of control and you can find the student's parent or guardian to remove the student, do so, but you still must protect your other patrons by alerting security and other library staff. Older students are much less likely to come to the library with a parent, and therefore your security staff and the police are the appropriate individuals to contact to manage threatening behavior. The U.S. Office of Personnel Management recommends creating a prearranged code word to use so your coworkers will know a situation is dangerous and you need help. Under no circumstance should you plan to confront or handle a ranting or threatening student on your own.

✳   ✳   ✳

To the extent that you can anticipate problems, from having more students requesting materials than you can accommodate to rudeness, you can create a plan of action to avoid or respond to these situations as they arise. Many of the problems regarding information services can be addressed in advance by coordinating with local school systems; some of the problems you encounter can be handled by arranging for volunteers to help handle the overflow and to provide assistance in specific subject areas. Treating students as if they are clients can help you respond effectively to those who are impatient with the information services process. Especially important is keeping them informed and allowing them to decide if they want to wait.

When large numbers of students gather, no matter what the age range, some behavior problems will arise. Establishing boundaries through posted rules and policies is the first step to preventing such problems. Other effective preventive strategies include circulating through the youth services area, showing interest in what students are doing in the library, and modeling appropriate behavior. When preventive measures do not work, along the same lines as effective classroom behavior management strategies, progressively more intrusive responses can be implemented to solve the problems, starting with nonverbal clues, such as catching a misbehaving student's eye, all the way up to private conferences with the student or, in the worst-case scenario, ejecting a student from the facility altogether. However, if you find yourself faced with a potentially unsafe situation, for the sake of your patrons' and your own safety, rather than attempt to diffuse the situation yourself, you should solicit outside help.

A final note: if a problem arises, especially with relational or behavioral issues, and the culprits respond to your intervention, remember to praise that response. These students have made an effort to cooperate; remember to make it worth their while.

EIGHT

Marketing Your
Homework Help Services

MANY OF US think a marketing campaign consists of television commercials, advertisements in newspapers or magazines, free samples at cosmetic counters, flyers on our windshields, holiday sales, web page pop-ups, dinnertime telephone calls, and mounds of virtual or "snail" junk mail. Whatever could any of that have to do with information services in general and homework help in particular? In reality, marketing is much more than one or another form of advertising. Basic marketing concepts involve how to connect consumers with products, from formulating the product itself to evaluating how successfully it meets the consumer's needs. In fact, most of the chapters in this book address one or another element required for a successful marketing campaign. Most librarians, in one way or another, are marketing all the time. As Stover (2007) writes, "If you're planning or implementing services, constructing Web pages, conducting needs assessments, promoting events or interacting with patrons, you're marketing."

Though library-specific marketing strategies are outlined in various texts and dedicated periodicals, basic marketing tools can be applied across all industries and services, argues information services marketing expert Christie Koontz (2004). The "marketing mix" has been the cornerstone of modern marketing since E. Jerome McCarthy first introduced the concept in the

1960s. "The Four Ps"—product, price, place, and promotion—constitute the marketing mix. In the case of homework assistance programs, the *product* is a conglomeration of every service you offer in the program (e.g., online virtual reference, formal tutoring, information literacy instruction, tech advice, online subject guides). Library services are funded via taxes, but money does not directly change hands between the library consumer and the service provider in a way the consumer associates directly with obtaining the service; the *price* of a homework help program consists of other costs to the consumer, such as the relatively high "cost" of the time it takes to come to the library or the low cost of a convenient website. The *place* of homework help is where students can access the assistance, both in the library and online: Is the homework help area comfortable? Do students enjoy gathering there? Is it arranged to facilitate work among small groups of students? Are sufficient technological resources available for students to use? Finally, librarians must *promote* the product; this is the main focus of this chapter.

Promotion is "the communication and public relations aspects of the marketing mix that inform the public about the product's benefits and applications" (Owens 2003, 21). Though many librarians may be uncomfortable with the process of formally "selling" their services, it is every bit as important as designing a good homework program. If students do not know what you offer, they will not use your services. For example, Connaway et al. (2009a, 8) found that nonusers were willing to try virtual reference services if they knew they were available. Dempsey (2009) points out that many studies show people request services, unaware that those services already exist in libraries. Some strategies are outlined below to help you create a successful promotional program for your homework assistance services so that students use the valuable resources you offer.

START PLANNING

As with all aspects of your homework program, avoid a haphazard collection of ideas and create a plan that includes consideration of your users, staff, facilities, and budget. Start by figuring out who will be responsible for developing the marketing plan and which staff members will be available to run various segments of the plan. Each promotional activity should have a manager or program coordinator to complete the follow-through, even if the same person fulfills that role for every segment of your program.

In the process of creating your communications plan, always include a budget rather than scrimp about for a little extra funding here and a little extra funding there. In the stressful economic times of the early twenty-first century, the temptation is to cut back on marketing budgets, but "this is the time to do more—and more careful—marketing and promotion. . . . In fact, if done right, these actions can even help your library save money" (Dempsey 2009).

A major resource in the planning process is your staff. Just as you should include the staff in the process of planning the various elements of your program, include them in the marketing plan, too. They may have ideas of how to use social media or what kinds of giveaways will be most appealing to your customers, and they will be integrally involved in implementing whatever plan you develop. Barber and Wallace (2010) recommend enlisting staff to market your services whenever they engage patrons. For example, as frontline staff help young patrons find what they need, they can recommend homework help services such as homework chat reference or formal homework programs, or they can offer patrons giveaways that include the program's URL. The power your staff has over what people think of the library cannot be overestimated. Fichter (2007) advises us that every employee "is a trusted spokesperson about the library in the eyes of the customer," and the impression that spokesperson makes, whether in a face-to-face encounter or online, often determines whether the user comes back. Every time a student interacts with one of your staff, your homework help program is being promoted.

ALA provides valuable resources to help you begin the planning process for marketing your homework help program. Most of the available ALA materials are directed at general library marketing programs, or the resources are discussed with specific constituencies in mind (e.g., YALSA or ALSC), but the concepts are easily applicable to homework help. In addition, "The Campaign for America's Libraries" and "@ your library" advocacy program materials contain toolkits that include marketing ideas to help you increase visibility and attract patrons. Programs tailored to specific types of libraries or services include "@ your library" materials for academic and research libraries, school libraries, public libraries, children's services, rural libraries, and young adult services. These resources not only contain advice but may have songs, artwork, giveaway suggestions, and other ideas you can use in your marketing plan.

Branding, a theme of the "@ your library" campaign, can be useful for your homework help program, too. The idea is to create a brand—a logo that patrons immediately recognize and associate with your service. This can be printed onto all publicity materials for the homework help program, such as posters, flyers, newsletters, and web links. Fairly soon, your customers interested in homework help will know that, when they see that brand, they will find support for completing their school assignments.

MARKETING RESOURCES FROM ALA

ALA, Marketing Library Services, link from index at www.ala.org/ala/profes
sionalresources/atoz/index.cfm

YALSA, Marketing Basics for YALSA Member Groups: www.ala.org/ala/
mgrps/divs/yalsa/aboutyalsa/marketingformembergr.cfm

New Members Round Table, Making Connections: Creative Marketing
for New Librarians: www.ala.org/ala/mgrps/rts/nmrt/news/footnotes/
november2008/making_connections_barry.cfm

@ Your Library Campaign: www.ala.org/ala/issuesadvocacy/advocacy/
publicawareness/campaign@yourlibrary/index.cfm

Getting Started @ Your Library: www.ala.org/ala/issuesadvocacy/advocacy/
publicawareness/campaign%40yourlibrary/prtools/gettingstarted.cfm

Kids! @ Your Library: www.ala.org/ala/mgrps/divs/alsc/initiatives/kidscam
paign/index.cfm

ALSC's @ Your Library site: www.ala.org/ala/issuesadvocacy/advocacy/
publicawareness/campaign@yourlibrary/academicresearch/academic
research.cfm

ALSC Kids Campaign Tool Kit: www.ala.org/ala/mgrps/divs/alsc/initiatives/
kidscampaign/index.cfm

School Library Campaign: www.ala.org/ala/issuesadvocacy/advocacy/
publicawareness/campaign@yourlibrary/schoollibrary/schoollibrary.cfm

Public Library Campaign toolkit access: www.ala.org/ala/issuesadvocacy/
advocacy/publicawareness/campaign@yourlibrary/publiclibraries/
index.cfm

Rural toolkit: www.ala.org/ala/aboutala/offices/olos/supporttoolkit/tool
kithome.cfm

YALSA's @ Your Library materials access: www.ala.org/ala/mgrps/divs/
yalsa/advocacy_final.pdf

KNOW YOUR CUSTOMERS

Throughout the needs assessment, planning, implementation, and training
processes, those who design and manage homework help programs must focus
on the characteristics and needs of users. If you are helping teens, you need
to be aware of teen culture and language; if you are working with elementary

school students, you need to know which toys, games, and music are popular with younger kids; and if you are offering information technologies, you need to recognize which are most attractive to and necessary for your users. Similarly, to produce effective promotional materials for your programs, you must speak so that your consumers hear what you have to say, and to do that you need to understand who comprises your "target audience" so you can select promotional tools that reach them effectively. For example, it does not help people looking for a list of library books on the Internet to hand them a brochure that tells them about your online catalog.

One efficient use of marketing efforts is "market segmentation"—dividing the market into groups with similar characteristics to whose needs you can respond and to whom you can address your publicity. This concept, popularized in marketing circles initially in the 1980s and '90s, is quite familiar to youth services professionals who "have long been in the habit of further segmenting . . . [the] youth services market by age and interest levels and then setting up collections, programs, and special displays to meet the needs of those market subsets" (Dimick 1995). The media tools and approaches you take to promote homework help services for elementary school students will be quite different from the choices you make to reach your teenage user population. In a list of aggressive marketing techniques for libraries, Sass (2002) provides an example relevant to homework help programs that reflects market segmentation. Because many older students often stay up late, watch lots of television, and procrastinate, Sass suggests,

> Develop creative PSAs [public service announcements] . . . designed to be broadcast during late-night television. "It's the middle of the night and you're working on a paper? Did you know that your library card will get you into the library's databases all night long? They're better than Google, and you can cite them, too!"

Similarly, because millennials spend a large amount of time online, it is worth maintaining a Facebook or MySpace page for your homework help program, and you might consider approaching your school district to see if you can post a link on school websites and online homework bulletins or grade posting programs if the district employs one.

For homework help programs, various segments of the student population are the obvious consumers—elementary school students, middle schoolers, and high school students; boys and girls; students from various racial and ethnic backgrounds. There are, as well, less obvious customer groups to whom you should market homework help programs. Teachers and guidance counselors advise students about where to turn for outside assistance with academics. School librarians see those who come to the media center after school for help and can direct those students who still need library resources after the building closes to your online or face-to-face programs. Parents and caregivers of school-age children often make the decision to bring students to the library in the first place, and parents of older students often select or suggest mechanisms to support their academic achievement. Remember: these are your consumers, too, and getting them on board with your program will expand the number of students who take advantage of what your library offers.

BE SEEN IN ALL THE RIGHT PLACES

In her thorough presentation on how to create and involve teen advisory groups, librarian Lisa Matte makes an important point about recruiting teen advisory group members that is equally important for your homework help marketing plan: for your promotions to be of value, you need to make sure your target group sees them, both in and outside the library. She suggests posting flyers near water fountains, in bathrooms, on tables in the youth services area, in books, and under the flap of photocopy machines. To reach young patrons, make announcements at all library-sponsored events for any subset of the student population. To reach parents and caregivers, make announcements at the library's programs for adults. If your library produces reading lists, the homework help information should be printed on these as well. Create displays for various sections of the library, and design screensavers for the youth services area computers.[1]

Not only should links to the various online homework resources be prominently displayed in the children's and youth services pages, but they should appear on the main page as well to attract teachers, school librarians, parents, and caregivers. You can create advertisements for your website, in the form of banners, "flyers," or videos, too.

Outside the library, ask yourself the same question you would ask inside the library: where do your target audiences go? Matte suggests setting up a booth at school functions such as school fairs and festivals or PTA/PTO meetings. Attendance is fairly high at school orientation sessions, especially for elementary and middle school students, so having a table at these orientations can put your program on students' and their parents' map early in the school year. Try publicizing your program in local businesses frequented by students, such as movie theaters, coffee shops, bookstores, mall food courts, candy stores, and health clubs that have a large teen clientele. The worst that can happen is a manager will say no if you ask to post a flyer or leave a stack of giveaways.

Using a prepacked portable rolling cart to provide services and information on library programs is an ingenious method of having your promotional materials readily available to take to any number of events. If you can secure school administrative approval to roll your cart of homework help and promotional materials to school fairs and athletic events, you will reach large numbers of students, parents, and school staff members.

GO CLUBBING AND PLAY WELL WITH OTHERS

Girl Scouts. Boy Scouts. Lions Club. Rotary Club. YMCA. YMHA. Boys and Girls Clubs. Homeschooling associations. These are all clubs whose membership includes at least some portion of your target audience, from the youngest children to parents and teachers. Make sure you get your message to these groups by visiting and leaving promotional materials, such as flyers and giveaways. When you visit and establish a relationship with a club or community group, you not only reach potential customers for your services but increase the chances that individuals affiliated with the organization will recommend your services. For example, a YMCA counselor might be more inclined to recommend the library's student research services to a student who comments on having a tough time with a research paper. Most of these organizations have websites, just as you do. If your library administration will agree to do so, suggest that you reciprocally link your websites. Then, for example, a father who goes to the Boys and Girls Club website to sign his son up for karate before he sits down to help the boy with his math homework will be reminded of the services you can provide for the latter task. The organizations with which you partner need to market their products and services, too, so the reciprocal relationship is mutually beneficial.

Considering that the entire purpose of any homework program is to support the formal education process, collaborating with local schools and homeschooling organizations should be a top priority. Not only do you learn about curriculum topics, assignments, and long-term projects by coordinating your efforts with the local schools, but posting information about your program at the school and in its newsletter confirms that your services are legitimate and relevant. Another benefit of creating a collaborative relationship with local schools is to get referrals to your program from the schools. When a student wants to learn more about a topic or, conversely, falters in class, schools have various mechanisms in place to address the situation, including, among other things, additional support during lunch or after school, "pull-out" lessons for one or a few students, remedial or enrichment programs, and recommended reading lists. Teachers who have information about your homework help program at their fingertips have one more tool to recommend to students who need or want to enhance the classroom experience.

Forging relationships with homeschooling organizations should be included in your marketing program. Homeschooled children benefit from highly individualized attention to their educational needs but may lack access to expensive resources and support systems for augmenting classroom learning. Homework help programs are an excellent resource for these students, but, again, they will use the programs only if they know about them.

CONTACT THE MEDIA

You may or may not have sufficient money in your marketing budget to buy an advertising spot on TV or the radio or in the newspaper, but you can certainly issue press releases announcing new activities, pitch a story idea to media outlets about your program, ask local media that cater to students and their families to run a public service announcement (PSA), and write letters to the editor about issues relevant to your program. YALSA has assembled samples of each on a web page to get you started.[2]

For the purposes of marketing your program, keep a file with current contact information for local radio stations, newspapers, and local organizations' or businesses' newsletters. The file should contain names of relevant editors or reporters at newspapers, such as those in charge of stories involving educational issues. For TV and radio stations, keep the name of the news director to contact about doing a story on your program and the names and contact information of public service or public affairs directors to contact for PSAs. At minimum you can send press releases to editors, reporters, and news directors, occasionally updating them about your services, and at maximum you might succeed in pitching a story idea to a media outlet. You might choose to send press releases to several news outlets at once, but stories must be pitched to individuals at media outlets and tailored to the news outlet's approach. For example, when you speak to an editor or news editor at Channel XX, you might note that the network frequently runs stories on how parents can help their children improve academic performance and point out that your story about the homework help services offered in the library dovetails perfectly with that priority.

For a news story pitch to be successful, it must have some kind of hook about something new or different that draws readers' or viewers' interest. For example, the upcoming implementation of a program pairing retirees from a local retirement home with students who need homework help or the installment of new special-needs technology equipment for students could be an attractive story to a local editor, but telling the editor you want people to know your homework program is still operating may be less appealing. When you send a news release or pitch a story, remember to include the critical basic information about the program and a contact person with whom the editor or reporter can get in touch to flesh out the details. Always follow up in a few days to see if the newspaper or news station will carry the story, and make yourself available for further consultation.

PSAs, which typically run fifteen, thirty, or sixty seconds, are usually shorter than a story, but they can be an effective way of getting across to your customers that you are available and open for business—if they reach your customers. Federal Communications Commission (FCC) licensure regulations require all stations to run PSAs, but stations handle them in very different ways, and you need to work with your local stations to find out the exact requirements. For example, both radio and television stations may suggest that you submit a script of a certain length to be included in the station's free community calendar each week or month. For television PSAs, you will have to submit the finished product, whereas some radio stations ask you to submit a script for the radio announcer to read. For television PSA ideas, search YouTube for "library PSAs," which will yield dozens of national and local library PSAs. The YALSA website noted above has sample radio PSAs, and at this writing the Information Network for Ohio Schools provides instructions for creating radio PSAs in an online toolkit.[3]

School-affiliated media outlets are equally if not more important than professional media. Students may or may not always read the *New York Times,* but they do read the school newspaper the instant it is distributed. A school's morning announcements or student-run high school morning news shows are strategically placed to reach the largest number of students who can benefit from your homework help services, but do keep in mind that students, especially in the upper grades, have been known to pay little attention to them.

HANG OUT ON THE INTERNET

There are three distinct advantages to using Internet and Web 2.0 tools for marketing purposes. First, just as you need to post flyers and announcements where your customers will see them in the real world, you need to market yourself where your customers go in the virtual world. As Stover (2007) points out, "[Technology] is largely responsible for today's marketplace trends, and it is also where librarians can find unique opportunities for addressing them." Several of these web tools are discussed below. Second, Web 2.0 tools, such as social networking sites and Twitter, have a viral, word-of-mouth quality so that in a split second your message can reach hundreds of contacts (Fichter 2007). Finally, the interactive nature of the tools injects your promotional materials with a certain legitimacy; because some of the content is created—and implicitly the rest is monitored—by your users, it seems more trustworthy to them. Connaway et al. (2009a) found that not only do students need to be aware of virtual reference services to use them, but they want a trusted friend to recommend them before they try them. This reflects a more general societal change in the United States to trust people who share one's personal qualities as opposed to putting one's confidence in experts, teachers, and others in the know. Fichter (2007) found that in 2003 only 20 percent of all respondents limited their trust to "a person like me," but just four years later that measure had skyrocketed to 68 percent. When you use Web 2.0 tools, even though you relinquish a certain degree of control over the content, you essentially invite your users to participate in the marketing process. Students are more likely to perceive other users in the same way they might view a "trusted friend," and therefore they may be more inclined to try virtual reference services at their recommendation. They know their peers will hop on to contradict anything they think is inaccurate or incorrect.

Some organizations recommend e-mail or texting for announcing upcoming library activities and programs. I advise against using texting altogether and suggest using e-mail only sparingly for marketing purposes. Texting is personal, and students use it exclusively to communicate with friends and family, though older people may use it for business purposes. I have heard many teenagers complain when they get unexpected, impersonal texts, whether from their cell phone service providers or, for example, from a daily joke service that sounded like a good idea when they signed up for it but now is just irritating. Similarly, students are as frustrated by impersonal promotional materials filling their e-mail in-boxes as adults. Unlike adults, who grumble as they click delete-delete-delete, students, who do not use e-mail for daily communication with their peers, often simply abandon an e-mail address that has too much junk mail. Thus, sending e-mail blasts is not likely to achieve your intended marketing goals.

Blogs

As part of the Web 2.0 interactive revolution, blogs allow you to create two-way conversations with your users and with other organizations and individuals.

Create a blog for your homework help program on which you post announcements, news, and tips for homework assignments, and your patrons can contribute their ideas and responses. You can make announcements to keep your patrons abreast of important concerns about schoolwork and improvements or additions to your services, and you can read other people's and organizations' blogs to find out what they are saying about you, to thank those who compliment you, to add or clarify information, and to apologize for any problems users encounter. This shows your library to be vibrant, active, and participating in the online community, which in turn creates loyal users. Schmidt and Houghton-Jan (2008) encourage librarians who respond to blogs to "speak in your own friendly and authentic voice rather than act as the voice of your library," but always to identify yourself as a library employee in the name of transparency and honesty. They suggest the following sites to find blogs that may mention your facility or staff: www.blogsbycity.com, www.blogdigger.com, www.metblogs.com, and www.feedmap.com. To find out who has linked to your library, they suggest typing the following into a search engine: "link:http:// (your library or program's website)".

RSS Feeds

RSS is an information delivery tool that can be tailored to a variety of uses including marketing. With RSS feeds, you can promote and make announcements about homework help events, schedules, or late-breaking news about the program's new features. Students who are interested in only certain segments of your program or certain subjects can adjust feeds so they receive information about only those segments. A student can get a reminder about when your tech volunteers will be in the building or an announcement that you have just updated your ninth-grade history subject guide. The disadvantage of RSS feeds is that they contain only small bits of information and cannot be personalized.

Twitter

Twitter is similar to a blog except it has a 140-character limit. It is most effective for sending time-sensitive messages, announcing special events, and touching base with your patrons, who can give you instant feedback. Marketers familiar with using Twitter successfully for promotion suggest uploading your photo, including links to organizations and websites of interests outside of your own organization, getting to the point of your "tweet" (Twitter message) quickly since you don't have that many letters to work with, and thanking people who follow you on Twitter whenever possible. If you begin to tweet, put your

Twitter name on various giveaways along with your websites and other contact information, and put it on your website.

Video Sharing

Fichter (2007) points out that, with more than 100 million video downloads per day, YouTube is too great a marketing opportunity to overlook. Dempsey (2009) suggests filming tutorials and instructional videos to post on YouTube to kill two birds with one stone: save valuable librarian time by illustrating, for example, how to use a particular search engine or access a database so librarians do not have to demonstrate these same skills over and over again; and create promotional material that illustrates what kinds of help students can expect and information they can access when they go to the library or use its website. She instructs library marketers to "choose one librarian who's not camera shy [to] grab someone's trusty digital camera, and shoot a 3–4 minute video." The professional quality of the video is less important than the fact that users can find it, learn from it, and appreciate your homework program for providing it.

Social Networks: Facebook and MySpace

Facebook, which began as an application open only to college students, and MySpace are unlikely to have many elementary school subscribers, but many if not most of your middle and high school patrons will have Facebook or MySpace pages or both, even if they created them at a friend's house or at the school computer lab over lunch. Your patrons' parents and teachers may also have social networking pages. For students with computers at home, social networks may be the major mechanism for electronic socializing, and many organizations—including libraries—have now created Facebook pages for children's and young adult services. For marketing ideas with these networks, start by looking at Facebook's marketing page (www.facebook.com/marketing/).

Although these applications are relatively new, many new books are being published on how to utilize various Internet mechanisms, including these social networks, for marketing purposes. Familiarize yourself with the options, such as forming groups for discussion purposes or inviting "friends" to join special groups, and decide which meet the needs of your marketing plan. Though having a Facebook or MySpace page potentially keeps your program on your customers' radar, to take advantage of the marketing potential here you need to be active, including information you know will be useful and interesting to students as they do their homework and engaging them in relevant discussions.

Also, don't forget to promote your Facebook or MySpace pages on announcements, giveaways, communication your local schools, and websites.

Google Advertising Grants

Many librarians view Google as a competitor, but imagine how advantageous it would be for your library if an advertisement for your homework help program would pop up in the search results when students went online and searched Goggle for homework help. If this sounds appealing to you, check out Google Grants (www.google.com/grants/), a program by the mega–search engine to provide free publicity for qualifying nonprofit organizations. Finding the right way to reach your target audience via Google requires time, effort, and knowledge. It is a challenge to profitable commercial concerns, which has led to the success of businesses that help companies with Google ad campaigns; certainly it would be challenging to develop a campaign for your library. However, if Google approves your grant, and you have the personnel and time to investigate this option and manage an AdWords account for you, it may well be worth your while.

BE GENEROUS: GIVE THINGS AWAY

People young and old alike love free things, and you should use that to your advantage if your marketing budget allows. There are two kinds of giveaways: those that are primarily useful to you because they allow you to mass-distribute information, and those that are useful to your patrons beyond enabling them to learn about your library programs. The former category of giveaways includes brochures, business cards, and flyers. Brochures should be colorful and use language that is accessible and appeals to the various age groups you serve. Business cards and flyers should be attractive, but by definition they contain much less information, perhaps the logo or tagline for your program that you put on everything related to homework help, telephone numbers, and the Internet URLs for your services. Bring these along whenever you represent the library at a neighborhood function, visit an outside group, or make an announcement about the homework help program at a library function. Typical giveaways that your patrons will continue to use in ways other than as a source of information about the library include pens, pencils, erasers, rulers, bookmarks, and magnets. Imprinted with your program's logo, URLs, the library's address, or hours of your services, they become walking advertisements for your homework program when your patrons carry them out of the library or pick one up at a school fair. Every time a patron looks at the eraser or the magnet, she will be reminded of your services. These are advertising tools, but don't turn your nose up at them; your patrons certainly won't.

ENLIST YOUR FANS

One of the best ways to expand the number of students who use your homework help services is to enlist the input of those students who already frequent your library, just as in the business world many companies involve customers in behind-the-scenes marketing programs (Stover 2007). Not only does this help you design promotional materials that are more appealing to your customers, it builds loyalty in your customer base and lends credibility to your program. If their friends are part of your program, it is all the more attractive to students who do not yet use your services. And if a student likes your program, you can be sure her friends will hear all about it.

Running contests for designing logos, writing a tagline, or creating other promotional materials for homework help services is one approach to use. Younger students, especially, enjoy having their artwork displayed, so another idea is to provide crayons, markers, and paper and ask them to draw pictures of doing homework in the library. Display the resulting masterpieces prominently in the children's section and online. Similarly, you can employ a kinesthetic teaching technique for eliciting older students' responses to academic material: hang large pieces of newsprint on the walls, give students markers, and ask them to write down what they think about the library's homework help resources, either anonymously or with their names; when the paper fills up, post a representative group of responses on your young adult web page or Facebook and MySpace pages, or use the most complimentary remarks as testimonials on promotional materials.

Another way to get your patrons involved is to ask them to help you develop a newsletter or blog for the program or create or star in a video about it (with written parental permission). Make sure room is reserved for children's as well as young adults' contributions.

In their book *Building a Buzz: Libraries and Word-of-Mouth Marketing*, Barber and Wallace (2010) emphasize the importance and power of asking satisfied customers to tell their friends about library services. Why not apply this concept to homework help services? Approach students who you observe coming to the library on a regular basis for homework help and ask them to tell ten friends about doing homework at the library. Promote this kind of word-of-mouth endorsement on homework help, children's, and young adult web pages. Perhaps you can create a form their friends can sign after they have heard about the program, and you can give little prizes to your most ambitious promoters.

How do you get students to participate in your marketing program? Walk up to them and ask them. Don't be pushy and make students feel cornered; they may never want to come back to the library. But you may be quite pleasantly surprised by how many students enthusiastically join your marketing efforts. Have a series of options available to discuss with them: contests or drawings, and some behind-the-scenes projects for students who shy away from publicity. The worst that happens is they decline.

In the process of asking students to participate in your promotional activities, you may get more than you bargained for. Some may complain or say they wish you offered different services than you have available. Every complaint or suggestion, however, is an opportunity to respond to your client base personally and to improve your services. If a patron complains that you never have any scrap paper around for students to use, and the following week you show that student the neat stack of scrap paper you rescued from the recycling bin next to the copy machine, you will have won a loyal fan. You have told the student that you are listening to him, that he matters to you, and that you will do your best to find solutions that work for him.

In the early twentieth century, Denver librarian extraordinaire John Cotton Dana recognized the value of marketing library services. Believing that the best way to win support for the library was to provide the services the local population needed and to make sure they found out about them, he included books in the languages his patrons spoke; he visited schools, churches, and newspaper editors; he gave circulars to newspapers; he published newsletters; and he won the good will of teachers by allowing them to take out large numbers of books at a time for educational purposes.[4] A century later, times have certainly changed, from the number of libraries and the demographics of the patrons to the nature of the information itself and the technology used to access it. Nevertheless, a well-planned marketing program that covers a range of promotional bases is still an essential contributing factor to a successful library or set of library services, including a homework help program. Gupta (2002) points out that "satisfying the customer is the primary concern in the marketing process" because your patrons will seek resources elsewhere if they feel your web page or the resources in your building cannot effectively help them. Worse, though, they will not even try your services if they don't know about them. Get the word out about your program through community groups, schools, traditional media outlets, the latest networking capabilities on the Internet, and good old-fashioned human contact.

When your marketing campaign is developed and implemented successfully, keep the bellows fanning the fire that fuels the planning process. Marketing is dynamic. Virtually everything that affects your homework help program will change over time: the students, technology needs, information formats, funding priorities, and the pedagogy that informs the nature of homework. Be ready to respond to those changes with tried and true techniques as well as new ideas so you can keep your customers satisfied.

Notes

1. Lisa Matte, "A Teen Advisory Group: What's in It for My Library?" Jervis Public Library, Rome, NY, www.jervislibrary.org/YAWeb/NYLAps_TAG.pdf.
2. YALSA's sample publicity materials, including PSAs: www.ala.org/ala/mgrps/divs/yalsa/teenreading/trw/trw2009/publicity.cfm.
3. Information Network for Ohio Schools, online PSA toolkit: www.infohio.org/PARENT/toolkit.pdf.
4. H. W. Wilson Company, "About John Cotton Dana," www.hwwilson.com/jcdawards/about_jcd.htm.

NINE

Evaluating Your
Homework Help Program

VALUATION, IN A sense, is the point at which implementing a homework assistance program comes full circle. A program begins with assessment, and it ends with assessment. It starts by assessing your clients' needs and ends by assessing how well you meet those needs. Many of the factors that inform the entire planning process—identifying the users, figuring out what the users need, determining how to meet the users' needs—are the very same factors that inform the evaluation process. Many of the techniques for understanding these factors, from focus groups and headcounts to surveys, are the very same techniques for conducting evaluations. This begs the question, if you have already conducted surveys, counted heads, and run focus groups, if you have created user-centered programs based on a good understanding of your patrons' needs and wants, why use valuable time and resources to do these things all over again in the name of evaluation?

In fact, *not* to evaluate your programs is what results in misuse of time and resources. As Robbins and Zweizig (1988) pointed out over twenty years ago, "[The] purpose of evaluation is to allow us to make better decisions about the library—to identify aspects that might be improved and functions that need to be speeded up or made less expensive." Assuming that the entire planning process to this point was effective, you likely created sound programs that meet all the requirements of students who come to the library to do their homework. But what if you failed to address key areas you thought were covered? What if one or another facet of the program is not working at all and you are wasting valuable resources on it and losing users? To keep such failing programs in operation is to do your library and your patrons a disservice. On the other hand, if your programs *are* effective, you improve the library as a whole, you increase the number of patrons who use your services, and you have evidence to support more funding and resources from the library budget. Without evaluating your programs, you can only hope that the latter rather than the former situation prevails in your library's homework help program.

Like every aspect of the program, when you evaluate you have a menu of methods from which to choose. What you select depends on the staffing, budget, and time you can allocate to assessment. All evaluation, however, must take place in the context of a plan that is incorporated into your homework help implementation procedures and provides data from which you can measure how well you achieve your goals.

From the start, you need to decide how you will use the results of your evaluation. Are you intending to use it to get funding? To confirm that, say, your subject guides are good resources for students, or to decide which online collections to expand? To determine whether you need more computers designated for student use after school—or at least to advocate purchasing more computers? To figure out how many staff members to assign to the floor? To prove that students use your facilities, both virtually and face-to-face? To select which methods will work best for your program, consider:

+ Which specific functions you will evaluate
+ How you will tie your evaluation to your program goals
+ Who will complete the evaluations, from the process of designing the assessment tools to interpreting the results of the data collected (e.g., specific staff members for each stage, outside consultants)
+ How frequently you will conduct evaluations

For any evaluation to be valid, you have to have a base against which you measure the change. You may have a fabulous homework fill rate now, but it may be exactly the same as the rate before you spent time and resources to improve the overall homework reference services. Students may gush about your menu of homework help services now that you have designed a program around their needs, their learning styles, and the curricula they use in class, but you won't have data to illustrate this success unless you have a base of comparison. Maybe students gushed equally as much about the services you provided before you started redesigning your program.

Another factor contributing to the validity of your measurement tools is sampling. In some instances you might choose to apply the measurement tool to every participant in one aspect of your program. For example, you might distribute a user satisfaction survey to every participant in your formal homework program and compile the data. But for many aspects of homework help services, especially for larger libraries, this is not practical. Taking a sample allows you to get equally valid information with less work and fewer resources.

To be fully valid, the sampling must be random. But sometimes it is just not possible to assure a random sample, such as when you ask students who visit your homework help website to rate their experiences. Only students who have convenient access to computers are likely to take the time to respond to your survey. Furthermore, if you have ever clicked on that little *x* to close a retailer's customer satisfaction survey, you understand why online survey sampling is limited: you get answers only from the students who are already invested enough in using your site that they *want* to let you know what they think, either because they are upset or because they care a lot about your product. It's a self-selected sample. On the other hand, as long as you recognize and acknowledge this limitation, online surveys may still provide useful information as you evaluate your services, even if they cannot provide a valid sampling for you to extrapolate information about your entire user population.

APPROACHES TO EVALUATION

Evaluations can be *formative* or *summative*. Formative assessments measure your homework help services as they are taking place. Summative evaluations measure what happens when the program is over or users are finished with the services.

Evaluations can also be *qualitative* or *quantitative*. Qualitative measurements draw on the opinions of those who use your programs. They are often called "soft measures," because they are less about numbers and more about feelings and perceptions. Print, telephone, and online surveys, interviews, focus groups, and user self-assessments are all qualitative evaluative processes. The aim of quantitative evaluations is to produce numerical data that measure effectiveness. They can be used to "measure a change in user competencies or behavior or to find correlations between library use and a person's academic . . . success" (Poll and te Boekhorst 2007, 33). An example of a quantitative measure is homework fill rate—the proportion of successful searches for information or library materials for homework use (Walter 2001, 10). The ideal quantitative measure for a homework help programs is the percentage increase (or decrease) in the GPAs of students who come to the library to receive specific types of homework assistance or use the library's website for specific homework assignments as compared with the GPAs of students who do not use the library. Typically, though, it is implausible if not impossible to access the data necessary for such a measurement or to control for various circumstances unrelated to libraries, such as economic and demographic factors and supplemental education provided by professionals or families.

Evaluations can measure *outputs* or *outcomes*. Walter and Meyers (2003, 90) explain the difference:

> Output measures are designed to answer the questions "how many?" or "how much?" Outcome measures, on the other hand, are intended to answer the question "so what?" You may have circulated 5,000 young adult books last year. . . . That is a basic output measure. If you wanted to know the difference those 5,000 books meant to the teens that check them out, you are in the realm of outcome measures.

Output measures include participation numbers or rates, such as how many students attend a class you offer on information literacy or how many hits you had on your homework help page in a given period of time. Outcomes-based evaluation—which is increasingly advocated in literature on evaluation in general and library services evaluation in particular—requires creating an assessment tool that effectively reflects the goals you established when you began the homework program planning process. It sounds daunting, but it need not be; such tools can actually be quite simple depending on what you are measuring. For example, when they evaluated the outcomes achieved by teenagers' participation in a formal homework assistance programs, Mediavilla and Walter distributed surveys with seven statements, each tied to an outcome or goal of the program. Students circled "agree," "disagree," or "don't know" after each statement, and room was provided for further explanation if the students wanted to elaborate. One goal was that young adults would "achieve educational success," and on the survey students responded to the statement "Working at the homework center helps me do well in school." Another goal—teenagers will "develop marketable skills"—was tied to the statement "I learned things while working at the Homework Center that will help me get a good job someday" (Walter and Meyers 2003, 94).

TYPES OF ASSESSMENTS

There is quite an assortment of assessments from which to choose as you plan the evaluation phase of your program. I discuss several in this section.

Behavioral Observations

Observations can be conducted by library staff, or you can hire a trained, outside evaluator. Behavioral observations can be used to determine how staff greet young patrons, whether students apply certain skills that have been demonstrated for them, or if and how students use the areas set up for collaborative homework projects. For example, the Monterey (California) Free Libraries hired an outside evaluator who observed the operations of a formal homework center (Brown 2002).

Focus Groups

Almost all of the literature about needs assessment and evaluation in libraries includes focus groups—small, representative groups drawn together to discuss specific aspects of the program. The teen advisory groups recommended for young adult services planning and development purposes are focus groups. Jones and Shoemaker (2001, 144) refer to them as "customer councils."

Children's areas should create customer councils, too, for planning and evaluation purposes. The idea that elementary school children are too young to participate in such groups is belied by the fact that many elementary schools have student government organizations with student representatives who communicate their peers' perspectives. Focus groups can also be developed for homework help service constituencies who are not the direct recipients of the services: staff, parents who bring their children to the library and may participate in students' education in other ways, and teachers who provide formal education. Focus groups are relatively inexpensive and provide immediate feedback. They are one of the few methods available in which users speak directly to you, the service provider, about their impressions and feelings. Focus groups do, however, require a trained facilitator to work most effectively. Additionally, some of the constituencies you seek to involve, particularly parents and teachers, may not be available to participate during library hours, and the groups are difficult to control. Sometimes one member's behavior can influence others in the group, and sometimes the conversation drifts far afield from the topic at hand. Verny and Van Fleet (2001) describe in detail the steps involved in designing focus groups for evaluation purposes.

Interviews

Interviews provide detailed information from the individuals sampled, and they are good for obtaining "soft" measures of how people feel about the library in general, homework help assistance in particular, and specific aspects of your program such as your website, the online collection, or tech tutoring. But interviews require a great deal of time to complete, since one or more staff members or outside evaluators must ask the same questions over and over again, listen carefully to the responses, and record what each person has to say. Then, once the answers are gathered, an evaluator needs to analyze what may be lengthy and divergent responses to the same questions and interpret how they are comparable. For example, to answer a question about how the staff treats students who seek homework assistance, one student might say, "I feel like they never have time for me and I'm just in the way," while another, communicating the same underlying concept that the staff does not always have time to answer students' questions," may say, "The people who work here are usually pretty busy and distracted, but if they see I'm waiting a long time, they always apologize and help me." An evaluator needs to be able to extract comparable information from these divergent answers.

Suggestion Boxes and Comment Cards

The old-fashioned request for anonymous feedback can be implemented in the library by requesting tangible comment cards that students slip into real suggestions boxes, or by creating a virtual suggestion box or blog on which students can share their perspectives on your services or specific aspects of your program. The advantage of this method is that students can give you their direct thoughts in their own words; paying attention to your customers' points of view is the essence of a good user-centric homework help program. You might find extremely good ideas about how to improve your programs or see your services from an entirely different perspective when you look at comments collected in this way. Still, the process of reading and evaluating the comments is time intensive, and the group who comments is self-selecting so you cannot extrapolate what you learn to the rest of your young patrons.

Learning Logs

Learning logs are journals in which students write entries to express their reactions to and thoughts about what they have learned. Students respond to general questions, summarize new concepts, write simple reflections, or identify what they did not understand. Though typically learning logs are not graded, they are valued assessment tools for teachers of all grade levels in that they show the extent to which students have mastered the material and how they think about the material. Their application to a library homework help program is limited, but they can be useful for formal classes conducted in the library. If, for example, your staff conducts information literacy classes for students or classes for parents on how to help their children get the most out of the library for homework help, a learning log can be a powerful evaluation tool. You can follow the progress for each student and for the program as a whole. In addition, you can extract both quantitative data (e.g., what percentage of students mastered the material) and qualitative data (what aspects of the material was most frustrating for the students).

Self-Assessment Outcome Surveys

Self-assessment surveys can be specific to conducting a particular task, or they can measure users' perception of their own growth. Poll and te Boekhorst (2007, 32) note that self-assessments are less reliable because users tend to overestimate the competencies they have gained. Because students may over- or underestimate their improvement attributable to the library programs in which they participate, it is a good idea to give a comparable survey to parents and staff members, too, so you can have several sources to validate the data provided by the students. An example of a self-assessment is the survey Mediavilla and Walter (2008) administered to evaluate how participation in the Monterey Free Library's formal homework center benefited teens, described below.

Tallies

Counting can help provide a picture of how well your program is doing its job by illustrating usage. Daily censuses, homework fill rates, desk counts, and website hits are all examples of tallies that can depict usage in your library.

Satisfaction Surveys

Surveys provide another avenue to "speak" directly to your users, with the added benefits of allowing the patrons some privacy as they make their views known and limiting the discussion to what you want to measure. Satisfaction surveys can be distributed to all your constituencies: students, parents, staff, and teachers. Questions can be closed, such as yes/no or true/false statements or scales to rate an aspect of a service. Questions can be open, too, allowing for more extended commentary. You can also categorize users by academic discipline or grade or age level, allowing you to figure out if your assistance is stronger in one or another academic subject or for particular grades (see Plosker 2002).

Surveys can consist of a few questions the librarian asks at the end of a homework reference query or hard copies of questions distributed to patrons. If you choose to distribute the survey face-to-face in the library, remember to pick times that are representative of your users' patterns, that is, a "normal" school week. I saw one recent student usage survey that was administered in early June; the analysts suggested that general usage patterns could be extrapolated from their resulting data. However, the beginning of June is the *end* of the school year; students are beginning to get restless, teachers tie up any loose ends in instruction, and if students are in middle school or above, classes are preparing for final exams. Data about student usage patterns during this frenetic state of limbo between school and summer vacation are hardly representative of patterns you will observe during the other months of the school year.

When you survey young patrons, keep in mind that as a rule students do not like filling out surveys and are unlikely to do so if the process is time consuming. Teachers experience this all the time when they distribute course evaluations at the end of a semester. One would think students would revel in the opportunity to tell their teachers what they could do better, but students simply circle a number on a scale rather than write anything in the space provided for comments. Jones and Shoemaker (2001), mindful of this preference, recommend that you "make it simple: What one thing could we do better? What one thing do we do right?"

COMBINING ASSESSMENT TOOLS

No single assessment tool is likely to help you conduct accurate assessments of all the services you offer as part of your homework help program. Ideally, you will find a combination of methods that works for your library. An example of how a library combined various assessment tools for a thorough evaluation is illustrated by Monterey County (California) Free Libraries' formal homework center evaluations in 2001–02. Mediavilla and Walter (2008) used the following combination of methods:

> *Focus groups* considered a couple of questions about ways to improve
> the centers.

Observations were conducted by an outside evaluator to provide a description of basic operations and location of the centers, including how they were situated in the libraries and how close they were to schools.

Staff surveys aimed to evaluate overall success as well as to find out how the programs impacted staff and the library.

Program coordinator surveys were designed to find out what the coordinators thought was most successful about the program and what obstacles they had to overcome to operate the programs successfully.

Parent surveys told the evaluators how parents thought the program benefited their children and helped them find out the parents' goals when they brought their children to the program.

Two student surveys were conducted. One measured basic use of and perceptions about the library and evaluated services generally; the other consisted of a set of pre- and post-program surveys to find out if students felt they were better prepared to do their homework after attending the program.

Daily census counts measured participation.

The Monterey County Free Libraries received a grant to conduct the homework center evaluation. Your library may not have the resources available to execute such a thorough evaluation consisting of multiple formats, but with the help of your staff and advisory councils you ought to be able to create a selection of assessment tools that will permit you to determine the strengths and weaknesses of your services. If you are struggling with funding or technical skills, one option is to include evaluation costs in any grant applications affecting your homework program. Walter and Meyers (2003, 90) report that more and more librarians are writing evaluation into their grant proposals, thus making it possible to hire outside consultants.

SAMPLE EVALUATION TOOLS

A sampling of assessment tools you could employ to evaluate the effectiveness of your homework help program appears below. The tools are organized according to the aspect of the program to be evaluated rather than by specific goal, because the specific goals need to reflect the needs of your particular population. Please note that this list is intended to be illustrative, not exhaustive.

Goals Related to Student Safety

+ Count the number of staff you have on the floor.
+ Conduct user surveys. Do students feel safe in the areas set aside for them to do their homework?
+ Observe the areas in which students work. Are adults wandering through areas where children gather, seemingly without purpose? How clear are the aisles? Are students well supervised?

Goals Related to Students Feeling Welcome

+ Conduct focus groups to address students' feelings about how they are greeted in the library. What does staff do or say to make them feel welcomed? Is there anything additional they could do? What do students feel about the layout of the homework help areas, and do they find the displays and signage appealing? Why or why not?
+ Conduct student, parent, and staff surveys to determine students' and parents' perceptions about how children feel about coming to the library. Conduct staff surveys to assess staff attitudes toward students who arrive for homework help and ways they are welcomed.
+ Conduct observations. Are children's and young adult areas separate? Are there areas for students to work collaboratively with their classmates? Observe the nature of visual displays. Do they include work by your young patrons? Do they reflect the diversity in your community? Are they colorful, which studies have found to be visually appealing to both children and teenagers?

Goals Related to the Physical Facilities in the Youth Services Areas

+ Count the number of Internet computers.
+ Calculate the seat occupancy rate (the number of seats occupied as a percentage of the number of seats available) to determine if you have enough, too many, or too few seats available.
+ Calculate the clustered area occupancy rate (the number of sets of seats clustered together to provide for collaborative projects actually occupied by groups as a percentage of the number of seat clusters available) and the table occupancy rate. This figure can suggest which kinds of work spaces students prefer to use and if your library provides them effectively.
+ Count the number of computers dedicated to homework during afterschool hours.
+ Conduct observations with a checklist in hand to assess features such as these: Is equipment up to date? What arrangements of chairs and

tables do you offer? Are the equipment and the youth services areas clean? Does the library have handicap-accessible technology stations and sufficient space for a wheelchair between the stacks and the desks?

Goals Related to the Effectiveness of Your Homework Help Web Pages

+ To determine whether your homework help home page leads quickly to needed information, create a relevant sampling of assignments and count the number of clicks required on the library website to find help with the assignments (Poll and te Boekhorst 2007, 89).
+ Count the number of virtual visits to the homework help web pages.
+ Without user participation, you or outside experts—for example, teachers—can conduct "cognitive walk-throughs," which involve performing tasks of an imaginary user (Poll and te Boekhorst 2007, 88).
+ With user participation, conduct web user surveys and focus groups. Ask patrons to do think-alouds while they use the library website or observe them while they use the website (requires students to access the pages while they are in the library).

Goals Related to Customer Satisfaction

+ Conduct focus groups. Speak directly to your patrons about whether they feel their needs are being met.
+ Use proxies, such as staff or teachers, to try out different services, such as technology in the building, the website, or the online collection. You can also use proxies to assess likely levels of satisfaction (Parasuraman et al. 1991, 338).
+ Conduct user satisfaction surveys. Design different surveys for students of different age groups, parents, teachers, and your staff to find out if students and their families seem to be satisfied with the services provided.

Goals Related to Effective Homework Reference Services

+ Conduct face-to-face desk counts, narrowed further by whether the queries are homework related or for other purposes.
+ Use daily reference tally sheets or logs. For example, the State Library of Ohio and the Ohio Library Council provide sample tally sheets and logs to constituent libraries. The tally sheets can be divided into "homework" and "other" for the purposes of measuring the output of homework-related reference services, or logs can be divided into subject areas or grade levels.

+ Conduct interviews with students at the end of reference interactions.
+ Conduct satisfaction surveys orally at the close of face-to-face encounters with students and online at the end of virtual encounters.
+ Use proxies who ask questions of the information specialists, either in person or online. The answers to the questions can be designed to reflect local curricula and common homework assignments at different grade levels and then evaluated for quality. White et al. (2003) used a similar approach to evaluate chat reference services, creating a set of questions designed to evaluate the quality of responses to different kinds of questions.
+ Outside virtual reference services often give you various choices of types of reports you can receive each month to measure the services they provide.
+ Examine transcripts of actual virtual reference chat to evaluate the quality of encounters. This approach, among others, is used by those conducting the OCLC "Seeking Synchronicity" project in which user patterns of virtual reference service are scrutinized (Connaway et al. 2009b). Among the purposes of the study are finding out how users determine service excellence, how they rate satisfaction, and how librarians determine success and satisfaction.

✳   ✳   ✳

The evaluation process is your system of checks and balances. You design, implement, and interpret assessment tools in order to find out if you are meeting your goals and the needs of the students who come to you for homework help, either in your library building or on your website. Like all stages of program development, the evaluation process you design is dynamic, and it must reflect the ongoing circumstances of your library, keeping at its core the goals of your institution at large and your homework help program objectives. You need to keep track of your program's outputs, which are more easily measured than some less tangible benefits of your services, but you should also determine whether those outputs make a difference to students. You might choose to implement a customer services evaluation model that emphasizes your patrons' satisfaction, you might focus exclusively on measuring outcomes, or you might decide on a combination of the two. During this process, consult the body of literature on evaluation models and their practical applications, a body of literature that is fast expanding in this era of accountability and economic downswing. The challenge is to choose a set of assessments that works for your library, your set of services, and your patrons.

Conclusion

I N THE PAST twenty-five years, burgeoning information technology and the Internet have changed everything about students' relationship to information, from where they access it to how much of it they encounter and have to synthesize throughout the day. A majority of students can find out what they want to know with the flick of a few fingers, twenty-four hours a day, from most locations in the United States if their families are among those lucky enough to have computers and Internet access at home. Another aspect of students' relationship to information has changed: it's not one-way anymore. At one time, students primarily received and practiced information that others chose to impart to them. Now, students IM, they blog, they tweet, they post on social networks. Their age and lack of experience are no longer barriers to widespread participation in the information network.

These changes have profound consequences for the future of libraries. So far, the predicted precipitous drop in library use has not materialized, and libraries have effectively evolved together with their adult patrons by automating catalogs, developing websites with online databases and electronic collections, and expanding choices for references services to include newer technologies like chat and IM. Library 2.0, though controversial, is widely adopted, and Library 3.0 is on the horizon. As millennials—kids who were practically born expecting information to be available when and where they want it—come into their own, the future of libraries may not be quite so bright. So far, young people still come to the library, whether in person or via the Internet, and often they arrive with homework assignments in hand. Youth librarians can create the lifelong library users of tomorrow by helping these students with their homework today. To do this effectively, you need to plan your homework help program well.

The first step is to find out what the patrons need. You should include them in the planning process and bring concerned constituencies—teachers, parents, and community leaders—to the table as well. Your frontline staff are one of your greatest resources, so keep them involved throughout the planning process and give them the training they want and need to make your program work. Select and continually update technologies that help students do a better job with their homework and, to the extent possible, select technologies that are compatible with the hardware and software at your local schools. Once you design and implement a homework help menu for your library that meets the needs of your users and the limitations of your budget, always keep the program dynamic through regular introspection and evaluation. If some service stops working well, revise it or drop it altogether and bolster the more successful approaches.

One of the most important steps you can take to ensure that your program is of maximum value to the students is to bring together school and library by developing and nurturing cooperative relationships with local school administrators, school librarians, and teachers. Traditionally the relationship between school and public library has been ambivalent if not adversarial, but it need not be so. In fact, the interests of schools and libraries are aligned with respect to students. Schools want students to use accurate information in their assignments and to learn to evaluate information effectively. Librarians can provide reputable sources of information and help bolster students' information literacy. Schools want students to do their homework, and the library provides a nurturing, safe, and welcoming environment to facilitate that. A cooperative relationship with your local schools helps keep the library collection relevant to support formal education and prepares you to provide homework help that meets the schools' expectations for their students. Teachers benefit because their standards are reinforced outside of the classroom and the resources available to their students are expanded. Teachers can also help you get the word out about your services. I continue to meet parents and students who are unaware that many kids can get the answers to a range of reference questions, receive individualized help with homework assignments, and get tutoring at the library—or that they can get help with homework, access the library catalog, and obtain full-text articles for research via the library website. These resources outside the classroom support what students learn in class. The bottom line is that schools want students to succeed, and so do you.

Along the same lines, a good homework help program brings together education and information services by incorporating sound pedagogical practice into librarian-student interactions. Modeling information literacy processes and scaffolding with techniques such as think-alouds help students master information literacy skills. When librarians respond to the different ways students learn, they maximize the support they provide to each young patron, and research about effective uses of praise in teaching can inform the way librarians help their patrons learn library skills.

Children's and young adult librarians can make and keep homework help program fans by giving students what they need but cannot get elsewhere. Students need accurate information and the skills to find accurate information by themselves in the future. They need access to the Internet after school hours, especially if they don't have access at home. They need help learning to use information technology effectively, and they need the freedom to practice navigating features of the Internet in ways that may not appear to be educational on the surface but develop skills they will need to compete in the twenty-first century. They need clear and simple instructions on how to use various library resources that may be new to them and homework help websites organized so they can easily access information the way they use it—by grade and subject. They need help with homework assignments ranging from a few math problems to major research projects.

Youth librarians can also make and keep homework help program fans by giving students what they want. Students want a comfortable place to gather and arrangements that reflect current pedagogical practice, such as places where they can work in groups without fear of reprisal for talking out loud. They want praise when they get something right and gentle instruction when they make mistakes. They want ways to access information that reflect twenty-first-century technology and society, including an online homework help presence and reference services in various formats.

The young people who come to your library, in person or online, are quite a diverse group. What they all have in common is that they are students and, by definition, are still learning. They are learning how to study, how to ask for help, how to analyze problems, and sometimes even how to behave properly. Most of all, they want to be welcomed in the library with warmth, patience, humor, and sensitivity.

Sources that Review Online Databases and E-Products

by Rose Nelson, Systems Librarian
Colorado Alliance of Libraries
Adapted with permission

Charleston Advisor—print and online journal

www.charlestonco.com (subscription based, but provides free reviews in every issue)
+ Reviews peer-reviewed by librarians, based on a scale of 1–5 stars. Individual reviews available for $35.
+ Rating system: content (audience), searchability, price and contract options. A composite score averaging these elements provides an "at a glance" rating, prominently displayed near the top of each review.
+ Reviews not only online databases but other products, such as virtual reference software and Serials Solutions' *360 Search*, a federated search program that allows patrons to search all your library resources with a single query.
+ Some recent reviews: Children's Lit. Comprehensive Database, January 2007; Teen Health and Wellness: Real Life, Real Answers, April 2007, 47–49.

Choice Magazine

www.ala.org/ala/mgrps/divs/acrl/publications/choice/ (subscription required)
+ Reviews academic databases; August issue devoted to reviews and E-Products for Academic Libraries Buying Guide.
+ Buying Guide includes short description of the product, the type of training the vendor provides, information about obtaining a trial, and what they base their pricing on, e.g., FTE, flat fee, concurrent users.
+ Previous reviews include Bowker, BioOne, Project Muse, ReferenceUSA, Taylor and Francis.

Databases: Peter's Picks and Pans

http://www2.hawaii.edu/~jacso/online-picks&pans.htm (from Péter Jascó, Library and Information Sciences Program professor, University of Hawaii)

+ Primarily reviews scholarly databases, but also some public library products such as the Gale Virtual Reference library.

Econtent Magazine

www.econtentmag.com

+ A good place to track industry news: research, reporting, news, and analysis in the commercial and enterprise realms.

+ Do a search on "database reviews". Reviews include Thomson Gale, Euromonitor, H. W. Wilson Children's Catalog.

Issues in Science and Technology Librarianship

www.istl.org/about.html

+ Reviews of scientific databases. Each issue has an "electronic resources reviews" section.

Library Journal

www.libraryjournal.com

+ Lots of reviews and RSS feeds. Categories of reviews include books, computer/media, reference, magazines, and Xpress Reviews.

+ Easiest to find the reviews by searching for "database reviews". Cheryl LaGuardia provides lots of reviews of e-resources.

+ E-reference ratings (2009) provided at www.libraryjournal.com/article/CA6707587.html.

+ Marketplace database reviews. Industry overview and future trends in online databases (2006) can be accessed at www.libraryjournal.com/article/CA6332160.html?industryid=47125&q=database+marketplace.

Library Media Connection (LMC)

www.linworth.com (subscription required)

+ Reviews some online database products, with focus on K–12 products.

LISTA: Library, Information Science and Technology Abstracts

Access via www.ebscohost.com/thisTopic.php?topicID=205&marketID=20.

+ Indexes nearly 600 periodicals, plus books, research reports, and proceedings.

Reference Reviews

www.emeraldinsight.com/info/journals/rr/jourinfo.jsp (Emerald Press subscription required)

+ In-depth reviews of reference works in topical areas such as philosophy and religion, social sciences, business, language and literature, area studies, and arts. Reviews some e-resources, but mainly reference monographs.

"Savvy Searching" column from *Information Online Review*, by Péter Jascó

http://www2.hawaii.edu/~jacso/savvy-mcb.htm is a list of references for the columns, some with links to the full articles.

+ Searching strategies
+ How search results are counted
+ Relevancy ranking and order of results
+ In-depth information on issues related to searching
+ "How Big Is a Database Versus How a Database Is Big," a great paper on understanding the difference between physical size, content, and accessibility of content.

School Library Journal

www.schoollibraryjournal.com

+ Range of articles on digital products, including databases. Search for "databases" and "digital resources" to find the most recent product reviews, including those by columnist Shonda Brisco.

Teacher Reference Center

Access via www.ebscohost.com/thisTopic.php?topicID=205&marketID=20.

+ Indexes over 260 titles including trade journals, periodicals, and books. Also includes reviews of e-resources.

H. W. Wilson Library Literature Index

www.hwwilson.com/Databases/liblit.htm#Index0

+ Provides indexing for over 400 journals, coverage 1980 to present.
+ Full-text versions for over 150 journals.

OTHER RESOURCES

Online Database Evaluation Checklist

http://warriorlibrarian.com/CURRICULUM/database.htm

Open Access Digital Library
http://grweb.coalliance.org/oadl/oadl.html
+ Portal of free full-text journals. A great way to supplement your collection.

Graphic Organizers

HAMBURGER MODEL FOR WRITING

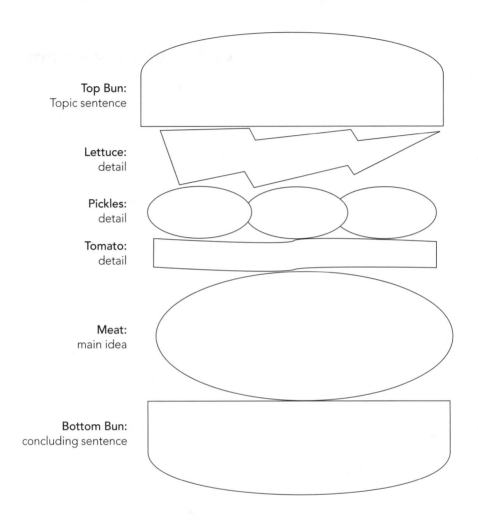

Top Bun:
Topic sentence

Lettuce:
detail

Pickles:
detail

Tomato:
detail

Meat:
main idea

Bottom Bun:
concluding sentence

Hamburgers taste better when we add the extras:
pickles, lettuce, and tomatoes.

Make your writing hamburger more interesting by
adding the extras: lots of details!

SEQUENCE ORGANIZER:
THE ORDER OF THE STORY

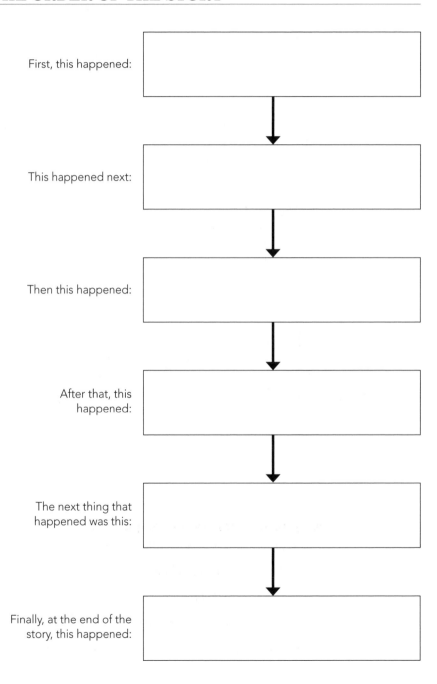

First, this happened:

This happened next:

Then this happened:

After that, this happened:

The next thing that happened was this:

Finally, at the end of the story, this happened:

BRAINSTORMING MAP

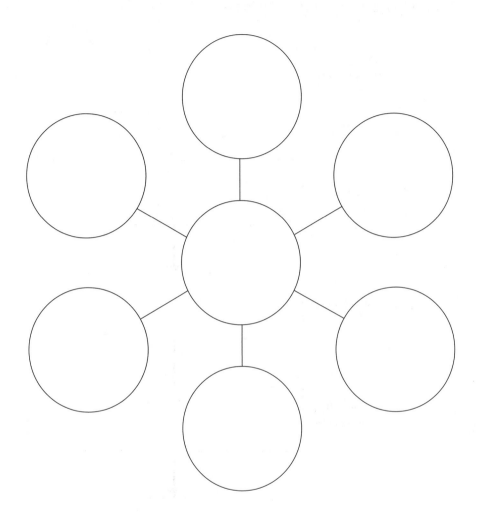

Write the main topic in the center circle.

In every circle connected to the center, write:

1. an example of your topic, *or*

2. a subtopic, *or*

3. a characteristic of your topic, *or*

4. a question you want to answer about your topic.

BLANK OUTLINE

I. _____

    A. _____

        1. _____

            _____

        2. _____

            _____

        3. _____

            _____

    B. _____

        1. _____

            _____

        2. _____

            _____

        3. _____

            _____

II. _____

    A. _____

        1. _____

            _____

        2. _____

            _____

        3. _____

            _____

    B. _____

        1. _____

            _____

        2. _____

            _____

        3. _____

            _____

SPIDER MAP IDEA ORGANIZER

TO ORGANIZE IDEAS: Write the subject you are investigating in the center. Along each "arm" of the "spider" write one subtopic of your subject. On each line for that arm, write one detail about that subtopic.

TO ORGANIZE WRITING: Write your main topic in the center. Along each "arm" of the spider, write one big idea about the main topic. On each line for that arm, write one detail about that big idea.

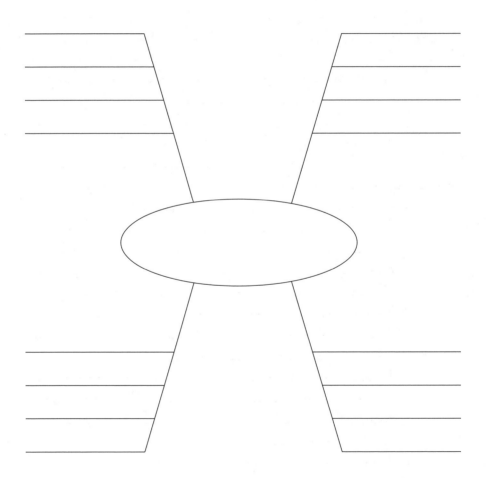

References

Abram, Stephen. 2006. Web 2.0, Library 2.0, and Librarian 2.0: Preparing for the 2.0 world. *SirsiDynix OneSource* 2 (1). www.imakenews.com/sirsi/e _article000505688.cfm.

AASL American Association of School Librarians. 2007. Standards for the 21st-century learner. American Library Association. Chicago. American Library Association. www.ala.org/ala/mgrps/divs/aasl/guidelinesandstandards/ learningstandards/standards.cfm.

AASL/ALSC/YALSA, Interdivisional Committee on School/Public Library Cooperation. 2004. School/public library cooperative programs. www.ala.org/ala/mgrps/divs/alsc/initiatives/partnerships/coopacts/ schoolplcoopprogs.cfm (accessed March 2009).

ALA American Library Association. 2009a. Library technology. In *The state of America's libraries*. Chicago. American Library Association. www.ala.org/ ala/newspresscenter/mediapresscenter/presskits/2009stateofamericas libraries/2009statelibtech.cfm.

———. 2009b. Supporting learners in U.S. public libraries. American Library Association. Public Library Funding and Technology Access Study. www .ala.org/ala/research/initiatives/plftas/issuesbriefs/learnersissuebrief09.pdf.

ALSC Association for Library Service to Children. 2009. Competencies for librarians serving children in public libraries. American Library

Association. www.ala.org/ala/mgrps/divs/alsc/edcareers/alsccorecomps/
index.cfm.

Anderson, Joseph. 2005. CIPA and San Francisco, California: Why we don't
filter. Webjunction, July 22. www.webjunction.org/cipa/-/articles/
content/432255?_OCLC_ARTICLES_getContentFromWJ=true.

Augar, Naomi, Ruth Raitman, and Wanlei Zhou. 2004. Teaching and learning
online with wikis. Presented at the 21st ASCILITE Conference, Perth,
Australia. www.ascilite.org.au/conferences/perth04/procs/augar.html.

Bailey-Hainer, Brenda. 2005. Virtual reference: Alive and well, reports of the
early demise of chat reference are unfounded. *Library Journal,* Jan. 15.

Barber, Peggy, and Linda Wallace. 2010. *Building a buzz: Libraries and word-of-
mouth marketing.* Chicago: American Library Association.

Bilal, Dania. 2004. Research on children's information seeking on the web. In
Youth information-seeking behavior: Theories, models, and issues, vol. 1, ed.
Mary K. Chelton and Colleen Cool. Lanham, MD: Scarecrow Press.

———. 2007. Grounding children's information behavior and system design
in child development theory. In *Information and emotion: The emergent
affective paradigm in information behavior research and theory,* ed. Diane
Nahl and Dania Bilal, 39–50. Medford, NJ: Information Today.

Bocher, Robert, and Mary Minow. 2004. Key issues for decision makers.
Webjunction, Dec. 13. www.webjunction.org/cipa/-/articles/
content/432235?_OCLC_ARTICLES_getContentFromWJ=true.

Boss, Richard W. 2008. "Open source" software. *Tech Notes,* May 8. Public
Library Association. www.ala.org/ala/mgrps/divs/pla/plapublications/
platechnotes/opensourcesoftware.pdf.

Braun, Linda. 2007. A waste of time and money? Posted on the YALSA blog,
Nov. 14. http://yalsa.ala.org/blog/2007/11/page/2/.

Brooks-Young, Susan. 2006. *Critical technology issues for school leaders.* Thousand
Oaks, CA: Corwin Press.

Brown, Jane R. 2002. Homework center evaluation 2001–2002: Evaluation
manual. Foundation for Monterey County Free Libraries. www.co
.monterey.ca.us/library/images/hwc.pdf.

Celano, Donna, and Susan B. Neuman. 2001. *The role of public libraries in
children's literacy development.* Mechanicsburg: Pennsylvania Library
Association.

Coffman, Steve, and Linda Arret. 2004. To chat or not to chat: Taking another
look at virtual reference, part 1. *Searcher* 12 (7). www.infotoday.com/
searcher/jul04/arret_coffman.shtml.

Cohen, Steven M. 2006. L2 ain't nothing without W2. Posted on Library Stuff
blog of Information Today, Jan. 8. www.librarystuff.net/2006/01/08/l2-aint
-nothing-without-w2/.

Collins, Mary A., and Kathryn Chandler. 1997. Use of public library services by
households in the United States. National Center for Education Statistics,

U.S. Department of Education Institute of Education Services. http://nces
.ed.gov/pubsearch/pubsinfo.asp?pubid=97446.

Connaway, Lynn Silipigni, Mary L. Radford, and Jocelyn DeAngelis Williams.
2009a. Engaging Net Gen students in virtual reference: Reinventing
services to meet their information behavior and communication
preferences. OCLC. www.ala.org/ala/mgrps/divs/acrl/events/national/
seattle/papers/10.pdf.

Connaway, Lynn Silipigni, Marie L. Radford, Timothy J. Dickey, and Jocelyn
DeAngelis. 2009b. Seeking synchronicity: Evaluating virtual reference
services from user, non-user, and librarian perspectives. OCLC. www.oclc
.org/research/activities/synchronicity/default.htm.

Connor, Jane Gardner. 1990. *Children's library services handbook.* Phoenix, AZ:
Oryx Press.

Coombs, Karen A. 2007. Building a library web site on the pillars of Web 2.0.
Computers in Libraries 27 (1). www.onlineinc.com/cilmag/jan07/Coombs
.shtml.

Cooper, Linda Z. 2004. Children's information choices for inclusion in a
hypothetical, child-constructed library. In *Information-seeking behavior:
Theories, models, and issues,* ed. Mary K. Chelton and Colleen Cool, 181–
210. Lanham, MD: Scarecrow Press.

Crothers, Laura M., and Jered B. Kolbert. 2008. Tackling a problematic behavior
management issue: Teacher's intervention in childhood bullying problems.
Intervention in School and Clinic 43 (3):132–138.

Czarnecki, Kelly. 2009. Spring cleaning with technology. Posted on the YALSA
blog, April 27. http://yalsa.ala.org/blog/2009/04/27/spring-cleaning-with
-technology/.

De Rosa, Cathy, Joanne Cantrell, Diane Cellentani, Janet Hawk, Lillie Jenkins,
and Alane Wilson. 2005. *Perceptions of libraries and information resources:
A report to the OCLC membership.* OCLC Online Computer Library
Center. www.oclc.org/reports/2005perceptiOns.htm.

Dempsey, Kathy. 2009. Five ways you can save money by marketing. *Marketing
Library Services* 23 (3).

Diggs, Valerie. 2009. Chelmsford High School's learning commons: From
program to facility. Massachusetts School Library Association. http://
maschoolibraries.org/content/view/609/294/.

Dimick, Barbara. 1995. Marketing youth services: Marketing of library and
information services. *Library Trends* 43 (3): 463–77.

Egan, Noelle. 2003. Young adults as library users: A review of the literature. www
.pages.drexel.edu/~nme26/ROL.htm.

Fayden, Terese. 2005. *How children learn: Getting beyond the deficit myth.*
Boulder, CO: Paradigm.

Feinberg, Sandra, Joan F. Kucher, and Sari Feldman. 1998. *Learning environments
for young children: Rethinking library spaces and services.* Chicago:
American Library Association.

Felt, Elizabeth Caulfield. 1999. Libraries are a lot like football. *Library Instruction Round Table News* 22 (2). http://fleetwood.baylor.edu/lirt/lirtnews/1999/football.html.

Fichter, Darlene. 2007. Seven strategies for marketing in a Web 2.0 world. *Marketing Library Services* 21 (2). http://infotoday.com/mls/mar07/Fichter.shtml.

Fidel, Raya, Rachel K. Davies, Mary H. Douglass, Jenny K. Holder, Carla J. Hopkins, Elisabeth J. Kushner, Bryan K. Miyagishima, and Christina D. Toney. 1999. A visit to the information mall: Web searching behavior of high school students. *Journal of the American Society for Information Science* 50 (1): 24–37.

Fisher, Doug, and Nancy Frey. 2008. Homework and the gradual release of responsibility: Making responsibility possible. *English Journal* 98 (2): 40–45.

Fitzgibbons, Shirley A. 2000. School and public library relationships: Essential ingredients in implementing educational reforms and improving student learning. American Association of School Librarians. www.ala.org/ala/mgrps/divs/aasl/aaslpubsandjournals/slmrb/slmrcontents/volume32000/relationships.cfm.

Freeman, Geoffrey T. 2005. The library as place: Changes in learning patterns, collections, technology, and use. In *Library as place: Rethinking roles, rethinking space.* Washington, DC: Council on Library and Information Resources. www.clir.org/pubs/reports/pub129/pub129.pdf.

Gagnon, George W. Jr., and Michelle Collay. 2006. *Constructivist learning design: Key questions for learning standards.* Thousand Oaks, CA: Corwin Press.

Gill, Brian P., and Steven L. Schlossman. 2004. Villian or savior? The American discourse on homework, 1850–2003. *Theory into Practice,* Summer. http://findarticles.com/p/articles/mi_m0NQM/is_3_43/ai_n7069034/.

Glasgow, Neal, Sarah J. McNary, and Cathy D. Hicks. 2006. *What successful teachers do in diverse classrooms: 71 research-based classroom strategies for new and veteran teachers.* Thousand Oaks, CA: Corwin Press.

Goldberg, Beverly. 2009. Nashville mayor wants city library to enfold media centers. *American Libraries,* January/February, 20.

Gross, Melissa. 2004. Children's information seeking at school: Findings from a qualitative study. In *Information-seeking behavior: Theories, models, and issues,* ed. Mary K. Chelton and Colleen Cool, 211–240. Lanham, MD: Scarecrow Press.

Gupta, Dinesh K. 2002. What is marketing in libraries? Concepts, orientations. *Information Outlook* 6 (11). www.sla.org/content/Shop/Information/infoonline/2002/nov02/whatsmarket.cfm.

———. 2006. *Marketing library information services: International perspectives.* New York: Walter de Gruyter.

Harris Interactive. 2007. American Library Association youth and library use study. http://ala.org/ala/mgrps/divs/yalsa/HarrisYouthPoll.pdf.

Houghton, Sarah, and Aaron Schmidt. 2005. Web-based chat vs. instant messaging. *Online*, July/Aug., 26–30.

Houser, John. 2009. *Open source public workstations in libraries*. Chicago: ALA Techsource.

Hurst, Susan, and Matthew Magnuson. 2007. Chat, email, and IM reference: School libraries and academic libraries, what we can learn from each other. American Association of School Librarians, American Library Association. www.ala.org/ala/mgrps/divs/aasl/aaslpubsandjournals/knowledgequest/kqwebarchives/v35/355/355hurstmagnuson_.cfm.

H. W. Wilson Company. 2010. About John Cotton Dana. www.hwwilson.com/jcdawards/about_jcd.htm.

Ito, Mizuko, Heather Horst, Matteo Brittani, Danah Boyd, Becky Herr-Sephenson, Patricia G. Lange, C.J. Pascoe, and Laura Robinson. 2008. Living and learning with new media: Summary of findings from the digital youth project. MacArthur Foundation. www.macfound.org/atf/cf/%7BB0386CE3-8B29-4162-8098-E466FB856794%7D/DML_ETHNOG_2PGR.PDF.

Jenkins, Christine A. 2000. The history of youth services librarianship: A review of the research literature. *Libraries and Culture* 35 (1): 103–140.

Jensen, Eric. 2008. *Brain-based learning: The new paradigm of teaching*. New York: Corwin Press.

Jeske, Michelle. 2005. The new service. *Library Journal*, March 15, 23.

Jones, Patrick. 2007. Connecting young adults and libraries in the 21st century. *Australasian Public Libraries and Information Services*, June. www.thefreelibrary.com/Connecting+young+adults+and+libraries+in+the+21st+century.-a0164421472.

Jones, Patrick, and Joel Shoemaker. 2001. *Do it right! Best practices for serving young adults in school and public libraries*. New York: Neal-Schuman.

Kafai, Y., and M. J. Bates. 1997. Internet web-searching instruction in the elementary classroom: Building a foundation for information literacy. *School Library Media Quarterly* 25 (1): 103–111.

Kelley, Tina. 2007. Lock the library! Rowdy students are taking over. *New York Times*, January 2, B2.

Kelly, Melissa. 2004. *The everything new teacher book*. Avon, MA: F&W Publications.

Kitsis, Stacy M. 2008. The Facebook generation: Homework as social networking. *English Journal* 98 (2): 30–36.

Koontz, Christie. 2004. The marketing mix: The 4-P recipe for customer satisfaction. *Marketing Library Services* 18 (1). www.infotoday.com/mls/jan04/koontz.shtml.

Kralovec, Etta, and John Buell. 2001. *The end of homework: How homework disrupts families, overburdens children, and limits learning*. Boston: Beacon Press.

Large, Andrew. 2004. Information-seeking on the Web by elementary school children. In *Information-seeking behavior: Theories, models, and issues,* ed. Mary K. Chelton and Colleen Cool, 293–354. Lanham, MD: Scarecrow Press.

Lenhart, Amanda, Paul Hitlin, and Mary Madden. 2005. Teens and technology. Pew Research Center, Pew Internet and American Life Project. www.pewinternet .org/Reports/2005/Teens-and-Technology.aspx.

Levine, Jenny. 2006. Everything you always wanted to know about RSS feeds, blogs, Wikis, social networking and gaming. Presented at the Illinois School Library Media Association conference, Nov. 9. http://theshiftedlibrarian.pbworks .com/2006Presentations.

Lewin, Tamar. 2009. In a digital future, textbooks are history. *New York Times,* Aug. 8.

Library Journal. 2005. Part of the solution: Judy Nelson—Pierce County Library System, Tacoma. *Library Journal* 130 (5): 529.

Loertscher, David V., Carol Koechlin, and Sandi Zwaan. 2008. *The New Learning Commons Where Learners Win: Reinventing School Libraries and Computer Lab.* Salt Lake City: Hi Willow.

Lupien, Pascal. 2006. Virtual reference in the age of pop-up blockers, firewalls, and service pack 2. *Online* 30 (4). www.infotoday.com/online/jul06/Lupien.shtml.

Manney, Erica. 2009. Insights from a library blogger. Posted on blog.tutor.com, Oct. 28. http://blog.tutor.com/2009/10/insights-from-a-library-blogger/.

Marzano, Robert J., Debra J. Pickering, and Jane E. Pollack. 2001. *Classroom instruction that works: Research-based strategies for increasing student achievement.* Upper Saddle River, NJ: Pearson Education.

McCabe, Jennifer. 2007. Learning Commons service model. James Madison University Libraries. www.lib.jmu.edu/edge/fall2007(2)/article2.aspx.

Mediavilla, Cindy. 2001. *Creating the full-service homework center in your library.* Chicago: American Library Association.

———. 2008. Lifting the blackboard curtain: The benefits of providing online homework help through public libraries. Presentation to the Queens Borough Public Library. http://ifla.queenslibrary.org/IV/ifla74/satellite-7/Presentation _Mediavilla.pdf.

Mediavilla, Cindy, and Virginia A. Walter. 2008. Out-of-school-time online homework help in California libraries: An evaluation study. California State Library. www.library.ca.gov/lds/docs/LSTAOSTEvalStudy.pdf.

Michaelson, Judy. 2009. Online homework help: Evaluating the options. *Young Adult Library Services,* Winter, 25–28.

Mielke, Linda. 2004. CIPA and Carroll County, Maryland: Why we filter. *WebJunction,* April 26. www.webjunction.org/cipa/-/articles/content/432245?_OCLC _ARTICLES_getContentFromWJ=true.

Meyers, Elaine. 1999. The coolness factor: Ten libraries listen to youth. *American Libraries* 30 (10): 42–45.

Morgan, Eric. 2009. Open source software in libraries. Musings on Information and Librarianship. http://infomotions.com/musings/biblioacid/.

Nahl, Diane, and Violet H. Harada. 2004. Composing Boolean search statements: Self-confidence, concept analysis, search logic and errors. In *Information-seeking behavior: Theories, models, and issues,* ed. Mary K. Chelton and Colleen Cool, 119–144. Lanham, MD: Scarecrow Press.

Nelson, Jennifer. 2009. Technology skills for 21st century librarians. Posted on the ALA Connect blog, May 5. http://connect.ala.org/node/73891.

Northwest Regional Education Laboratory. 2005. Classroom examples—primary: Thinking Aloud. www.netc.org/focus/examples/thinki.php.

Owens, Irene. 2003. *Strategic marketing in library and information science.* New York: Routledge.

Parasuraman, A., Leonard L. Berry, and Valerie A. Zeithaml. 1991. Perceived service quality as a customer-based performance measure: An empirical examination of organizational barriers using an extended service quality model. *Human Resource Management,* Fall, 335–364.

Plosker, George R. 2002. Conducting user surveys: An ongoing information imperative. *Online* 26 (5). www.infotoday.com/ONLINE/sep02/Plosker.htm.

Poll, Roswith, and Peter te Boekhorst. 2007. *Measuring quality: Performance measurement in libraries.* The Hague: IFLA Publiciations.

Powell, Alvin. 2007. How Sputnik changed U.S. education. *Harvard University Gazette.* Harvard University. http://news.harvard.edu/gazette/story/2007/10/how-sputnik-changed-u-s-education.

Power, Effie. 1930. *Library service for children.* Chicago: American Library Association.

Radford, Marie L., and Joseph Thompson. 2004. Yo dude! Y r u typin so slow? Interpersonal communication in chat reference service encounters. Paper presented at the Virtual Reference Desk 6th Annual Conference, Nov. 8–9, Cincinnati, Ohio. www.webjunction.org/c/document_library/get_file?folderId=440523&name=DLFE-11770.pdf.

Radford, Marie L., and Lynn Silipigni Connaway. 2008. Getting better all the time: Improving communication and accuracy in virtual reference. Presented at the Bibliographical Center for Research's Reference Renaissance, Aug. 4–5, Denver, CO. www.bcr.org/reference renaissance/2008/presentations.html.

Rainie, Lee. 2006. Digital natives: How today's youth are different from their "digital immigrant" elders and what that means for libraries. Presentation to the Metropolitan New York Library Council, Oct. 27, Brooklyn. Pew Internet and American Life Project. www.pewinternet.org/Presentations/2006/Digital-Natives-How-todays-youth-are-different-from-their-digital-immigrant-elders-and--w.aspx.

———. 2009. Networked learners. Keynote presentation to Michigan Virtual University, Dec. 2. Pew Internet and American Life Project. www.slideshare.net/PewInternet/networked-learners-mvu-keynote.

Rathbone, Josephine A. 1901. Cooperation between libraries and schools: An historical sketch. *Library Journal* 26 (April): 187–191.

Robbins, Jane, and Douglas Zweizig. 1988. Are we there yet? Evaluating library collections, reference services, programs, and personnel. *American Libraries* 16 (10): 724–727.

Roe, Betty D., Barbara D. Stoodt-Hill, and Paul C. Burns. 2007. *Secondary school literacy instruction: The content areas.* Boston: Houghton Mifflin.

Ross, Mary Bucher. 2002. Focus on learners: Tips for technology training. *CLENExchange* 19 (1). www.ala.org/ala/mgrps/rts/clenert/newsletter/0902 .pdf.

Rubin, Richard E. 2001. Measuring organizational effectiveness. In *Library evaluation: A casebook and can-do guide,* Danny P. Wallace and Connie Van Fleet, 11–24. Englewood, CO: Libraries Unlimited.

RUSA Reference and User Services Association. 2004. Guidelines for implementing and maintaining virtual reference services. *Reference and User Services Quarterly* 33 (1): 9–13.

RUSA Reference and User Services Association and YALSA Young Adult Library Services Association. 2008. Guidelines for library services to teens, ages 12–18. American Library Association. http://yalsa.ala.org/guidelines/ referenceguidelines.pdf.

Sass, Rivkah K. 2002. Marketing the worth of your library. *Library Journal,* June 15. http://libraryjournal.reviewsnews.com/index.asp?layout=article&article Id=CA220888.

Sayers, Frances Clarke. 1963. The American origins of public library work with children. *Library Trends* 12 (July): 6–12.

Schmidt, Aaron, and Sarah Houghton-Jan. 2008. How to drive traffic to your website. *Marketing to Library Services* 22 (6). www.infotoday.com/mls/ nov08/Schmidt_Houghton-Jan.shml.

Sealander, Judith. 2003. The failed century of the child: Governing America's young in the twentieth century. New York: Cambridge University Press.

Shenton, Andrew. 2007. Causes of information-seeking failure: Some insights from an English research project. In *Youth information-seeking behavior: Context, theories, models and issues,* ed. Mary K. Chelton and Colleen Cool, 313–364. Lanham, MD: Scarecrow Press.

Silver, Harvey F., Richard W. Strong, and Matthew J. Perini. 2000. *So each may learn: Integrating learning styles and multiple intelligences.* Alexandria, VA: Association for Supervision and Curriculum Development.

Stephens, Michael. 2006. Web 2.0 and libraries: Best practices for social software. Posted on ALA TechSource blog. www.alatechsource.org/ltr/web-20-and -libraries-best-practices-for-social-software.

St. Lifer, Evan. 2001. What public libraries must do to survive. *Library journal,* April 1. www.libraryjournal.com/article/CA74712.html.

Stover, Jill. 2007. What's marketing got to do with it? WebJunction, June 5. www .webjunction.org/marketing/articles/content/444514.

Sullivan, Michael. 2005. *Fundamentals of children's services*. Chicago: American Library Association.

Thompson, Julia G. 1998. *Discipline survival kit for the secondary teacher*. San Francisco: Jossey-Bass.

Thompson, Susan, M., ed. 2008. *Core technology competencies for librarians: A LITA Guide*. New York: Neal-Schuman.

Tileston, Donna Walker. 2004. *What every teacher should know about learning, memory, and the brain*. Thousand Oaks, CA: Corwin Press.

U.S. Office of Personnel Management. 1998. Workplace security, in *Dealing with workplace violence: A guide for agency planners*. www.opm .gov/Employment_and_Benefits/WorkLife/OfficialDocuments/ handbooksguides/WorkplaceViolence/p3-s5.asp.

Vaillancourt, Renee J. 2000. *Bare bones young adult services: Tips for public library generalists*. Chicago: American Library Association.

Valenza, Joyce Kasman. 2007. "It'd be really dumb not to use it": Virtual libraries and high school students' information seeking and use. A focus group investigation. In *Youth information-seeking behavior: Context, theories, models and issues,* vol. 2, ed. Mary K. Chelton and Colleen Cool, 207–256, Lanham, MD: Scarecrow Press.

Verny, Roger, and Connie Van Fleet. 2001. Conducting focus groups. In *Library evaluation: A casebook and can-do guide*, ed. Danny P. Wallace and Connie Van Fleet, 43–51. Englewood, CO: Libraries Unlimited.

Wallace, Raven McCrory, Jeff Kuperman, Joseph Krajcik, and Elliot Soloway. 2000. Science on the Web: Students online in a sixth grade classroom. *Journal of the Learning Sciences* 9 (1): 75–104.

Walter, Virginia A. 2001. *Children and libraries: Getting it right*. Chicago: American Library Association.

Walter, Virgina A. 2003. Public library service to children and teens: A research agenda. *Library Trends,* Spring 2003.

Walter, Virginia A., and Cindy Mediavilla. 2005. Teens are from Neptune, librarians are from Pluto: An analysis of online reference transactions. *Library Trends* 54 (2): 209–224.

Walter, Virginia A., and Elaine Meyers. 2003. *Teens and libraries: Getting it right*. Chicago: American Library Association.

Webb, Adam. 2005. Problem patron policies in public libraries: A content analysis. MLS diss., University of North Carolina at Chapel Hill. http://etd .ils.unc.edu/dspace/bitstream/1901/188/1/apwebb.pdf.

White, Marilyn Domas, Eileen G. Abels, and Neal Kaske. 2003. Evaluation of chat reference service quality. *D-Lib Magazine* 9 (2). www.dlib.org/dlib/ february03/white/02white.html.

Willet, Holly G. 1995. *Public library youth services: A public policy approach*. Norwood, NJ: Ablex Publishing Corporation.

Woolls, Blanche. 2003. Children's libraries and librarians. In *The Encyclopedia of library and information science,* vol. 2, ed. Miriam Drake, 522–530. New York: CRC Press.

YALSA Young Adult Library Services Association. 2010. YALSA's Competencies for Librarians Serving Youth. American Library Association. http://www .ala.org/ala/mgrps/divs/yalsa/profdev/yadeservethebest_201.pdf.

Index